(DEUS NON FORTUNA)

Kate Tyrrell
'Lady Mariner'

To Kate (Nora)
with sincerest thanks

As Kate would say
every Fault is a fashion
From John Mahon
L2 OAKLANDS
ARKLOW
CO. WICKLOW

Nora you
are special

Kate Tyrrell
'Lady Mariner'

The story of the extraordinary woman who sailed the *Denbighshire Lass*

John Mahon

Basement Press
DUBLIN

Copyright © John Mahon 1995

First published in Ireland in 1995 by
Basement Press
an imprint of Attic Press Ltd
29 Upper Mount Street
Dublin 2.

A catalogue record for this title is available from the British library.

ISBN 1 85594 140 6

Cover Design: Michael O'Dwyer
Setting: Jimmy Lundberg Desktop Publishing
Printing: The Guernsey Press Co. Ltd

This book is published with the financial assistance of the Arts Council/An Chomhairle Ealaíon, Ireland.

To my mother,
Elizabeth Lily Fitzpatrick (Mahon),
and my grandmother, Kate Tyrrell.

We are sailing away with the wind and the tide,
Our hopes and hearts riding high,
Away to the west where the sun goes to rest,
And there our destinies lie.

Elizabeth (Lily Fitzpatrick) Mahon 1964.

Contents

ACKNOWLEDGEMENTS

Many people have helped me to compile this short book. Some of them I know do not wish to be named: to them, I can only give my sincerest thanks.

I am extremely grateful to the staff of *Sea Breezes* magazine, without whom I could not have started to write at all.

To Gregory O'Connor, archivist of the National Archives, Ireland, who was so helpful, my sincere thanks.

Appreciation to Tom Coppack, who was one of the first to correspond with me after I contacted him through *Sea Breezes*. Sadly, he has now passed away. Rest in peace. Thanks also to all the local people of the Maritime Museum, Arklow, and the various members of the Tyrrell families in Arklow who helped me with my queries on many occasions.

Thanks to Jim Dixon of Arklow who had so many memories to relate to me.

Special thanks to all the Wexford people, relatives of John's mother, including Ann Brennan, who was so helpful, and, especially, Mrs Kathleen Kinsella, Pat Brennan's daughter, and all her family and relations, including Tom Gregory, Cron Cribín, Inch, Gorey, who proved invaluable.

Thanks for all the help I was given in locating headstones in Wexford graveyards, and in tracing records of births and deaths. These people I know would rather remain anonymous. Special thanks to some people who have now passed away from this life, but who were so helpful: Mr Joe Colvin, who was full of relevant dates and facts, Mr J. Cullen, Ferrybank, Arklow, who was one of the first to show me Kate's name documented on shipping registers.

Thanks to Ned Sweeney, Arklow, Co. Wicklow, for his assistance.

Thanks to Colm Barn, Cahore, for all his assistance.

Thanks to Mr J. Murphy, Courtown Harbour, for all his assistance and time. Also special thanks to someone in my workplace who kept at me to compile this story.

Special thanks to my typist who had to decipher my writing.

If I were to list all the correspondents from various institutions who helped me, the list would be endless. All I can say to these people is thank you.

Very special thanks to C. McCarthy, Point House, Point Road, Dundalk, Co. Louth, who furnished me with maritime data information, and to Dick Scott, St James's Court, Ennis Road, Limerick, and Tony Price of Lamberton, Arklow, all of whom were of invaluable assistance. And likewise John Tyrrell of Arklow Marine Services and his father Willie Tyrrell, who recently passed away. Rest in peace. All of this family were extremely helpful.

Gratitude also to the scores of people I spoke to at different shipping locations, and who gave me invaluable information. Very special thanks to one of the greatest photographers I'll probably ever meet, Mr Pat Doran, Aske, Gorey, Co. Wexford, to whom I gave the unenviable task of photographing a painting of the *Denbighshire Lass* and also of enlarging a print of the ship which I had acquired on microfilm. Both these tasks he carried out expertly. I am forever in his debt. Many thanks also to his wife Mary for her hospitality.

There are so many people in the Arklow area whom I

would like to thank. Most of these would probably be embarrassed if I were to have their names printed. Special thanks also to one of my friends who assisted me and continually told me during my researches that my family ship the *Denbighshire Lass* must have been a 'Marie Celeste phantom ship'. But he was of invaluable assistance. He also wishes to remain unlisted.

Gratitude to so many people in the area of Co. Wexford: Cron Cribín, Baker's Cross, Moneygarrow, Castletown and Ballycanew. All these Wexford people were an inspiration. I am forever in their debt.

And my very special thanks to Stephen Mahon and Ronan Mahon who were the first to read my story in its infancy. Their opinions on all aspects were most essential and inspirational.

I would place emphasis on the fact that all the various people I looked to for assistance and guidance are in no way responsible for whatever is in the final book. All mistakes are my own, and entirely my responsibility.

Sincerest thanks also to Father Walter Forde and all the staff of *Link* magazine in Gorey, Co. Wexford, who were more than helpful and so thoughtful.

Very special appreciation to another lady who was an acquaintance of mine – Sister Evangelista, of Arklow Convent, who was a major inspiration for this story. Sadly she has now passed away. May she rest in peace.

Special thanks to another member of the family dynasty who always gave me great and detailed information, usually followed by a warning that 'You should not be digging up all these stories. They should be let rest.'

Finally, thanks to my wife Irene for everything, and, once again, wholehearted thanks to my son Stephen for his input into this story, and to my son Ronan for his work in searching through mountains of archives, records and shipping documents.

The author would like to thank the following for their generous help in making this book possible:

Arklow Shipping, North Quay, Arklow, Co. Wicklow.

Pressure Hydraulics, Centaur Street, Carlow.

Arklow UDC, Town Hall, Arklow.

ISO Engineering Ltd, Bridges Industrial Estate, Naas Road, Dublin.

Cyril McLoughlin.

Patricia Ryan.

Tony Nolan.

Gary Ryan.

Liam Prendergast.

Ciaran O'Reilly.

Modern Plant, Otter House, Naas Road, Clondalkin, Dublin.

Foodenge Ltd, Unit 19, Phase 2, Western Industrial Estate, Naas Road, Dublin.

IFI – Irish Fertilizer Industries, Arklow, Co. Wicklow.

Peter Power, 1 Lower Main Street, Arklow.

John Tyrrell, Arklow.

Billy Tyrrell, Arklow.

Matthew Wall & Sons Ltd, Bosheen, New Ross, Co. Wexford.

E. Fox Engineers Ltd, Herberton Road, Crumlin, Co. Dublin.

Rotate Ltd, 136 Slaney Close, Dublin Industrial Estate, Dublin.

Noel McLoughlin.

Mary Hughes.

Tina Brady.

Noel Ryan.

Theresa Dalton.

South Eastern Refrigeration, Thomas Hill, Waterford.

Arklow Garden of Ireland Festival Committee (13-16 July).

Atlas Copco (Ireland) Ltd.

Flomeaco Co. Ltd, Main Street, Clane, Co. Kildare.

John English of Murphy Engineers Ltd, JFK Avenue, Dublin 12.

Waterford Foods PLC, Inch, Gorey, Co. Wexford.

AUTHOR'S NOTE

Kate Tyrrell, 'Lady Mariner' is a work of non-fiction, based on my own research in archives, museums, shipping records and among my own relatives and friends. However, as with any biography, sometimes, despite all the information one obtains and the stories one hears, some conjecture is necessary for the writer.

As a young boy growing up in Arklow I was always fascinated by the world of shipping – and still am, land-lubber though I am. Merchant seamen live in a different world to the rest of us, and sea-going people are an entire-ly different breed. The sea gets into the blood and takes hold of you for life.

Growing up, the stories I heard usually centred on the family ships. Granted, some of them were astounding. I was told that schooners like the *Denbighshire Lass* sailed from Merseyside, hugging the coast of France, then Spain, the sailing down towards Morocco and around the coast of Africa via Sierra Leone and the Ivory Coast before finally reaching Cape Hope. The ships would then veer west-wards towards the Tristan da Cunha islands with cargoes of food for the British colonies there. The hazards of such a trip, in the seemingly fragile wooden ships so different from the huge metal hulks of today, are difficult for us to comprehend. Later, when I was researching this book, I spoke to some very experienced sailors who travelled around Cape Horn. Their stories were hair-raising to say the least. Many of them I have recorded on tape to keep for posterity.

It would have been completely impossible to write anything on this subject, I feel, if I had not been born in a seafaring town like Arklow. There is so much history attached to all local towns in the area. I came to know the connection of Kate Tyrrell's husband, John, who lived in Inch, Gorey, Co. Wexford – in fact I now work in the area. I am so pleased to be part of them all. Wexford people are very special. The Wexford connection had an enormous input into this book. Of course, because this story took place so long ago, most of the people involved have since passed on, but I have done what I can.

I listened to all the stories of the *Denbighshire Lass* and attempted to fit the pieces together into a coherent history that would tell the story of this ship and the extraordinary woman who controlled her. A pure log of dates and voyages would have made tedious reading, and in fact so much historical information was missing that this would have been impossible. My research for this book also brought me into contact with sources as far afield as the UK, the Canadian Maritime History Archives in Newfoundland, the Dublin Archives, Courtown Harbour, and many maritime establishments. So *Kate Tyrrell, 'Lady Mariner'* must be taken for what it is: a book founded on fact and compiled from stories.

It is also, I hope, an insight into the life of a young woman who was decades ahead of her time: a mariner and a businesswoman. As I wrote, the dynamic Kate Tyrrell began to take over the story. I have attempted to keep the tale simple and straightforward.

INTRODUCTION

I was born in Arklow, a town with a rich maritime history. Shipping has been the life of the town for generations. Most of my youth was spent down at Arklow Harbour, and, after school, on the various fishing boats. It was a wonderful haunt for a young boy and his mates. We would collect fish from the boats and stare in fascination at the winches, trawl boards and, of course, if we were shown the wheelhouse or the echo sounder it would be a bonus. It was around 1957 and I was unaware that so much of the shipping world was changing for ever.

When we were not at play around the harbour or gallivanting on the beach, we would make our way to an old ruined factory, Kynochs, on the opposite side of the harbour. There we would dig up a cotton-wool substance known as gun cotton, dry it out, stuff it in a tin can, light it with a fuse and wait until it exploded. This old munitions factory (now almost completely gone) was a massive building and stretched for what seemed to us to be miles, from Arklow Harbour out to where the caravan park now stands. There were thousands of stories about this factory. Arklow has a bridge with nineteen arches – and a final one some twenty feet from the last one, said to have been built by Kynochs to bring water to the factory. Not that such information interested us at the time – we were far too busy playing in the vast ruins.

But our minds were always on the harbour, and towards evening we would drift back there. At that time there were old wrecks and parts of ships in the middle of the river.

They looked to me as if they had been there since the beginning of time. I was told that they were the wrecks of sailing ships of years before – and I found it difficult to imagine them sailing down the Avoca near Kynochs.

I first became aware of a most formidable lady, known as Kate Tyrrell, in 1957, when my mother Lily, Kate's own daughter, told me her story. From then on I heard everything I could about her. Not only was Kate the owner of the first schooner to fly the Irish tricolour in Britain, she was, uniquely among woman, a capable sailor who ably navigated the schooner herself and ran all aspects of the family nautical business, including navigation, ship repairs and the business and administration side of the company.

I learned that Kate was a most remarkable and forward-looking idealist. She would leave no stone unturned in her search for the best; she was always self-sufficient, and she always had her eyes on the future. She was quick to solve problems, her acute business mind seeing immediately what needed to be done. She was alert and surefooted, capable of dominating any discussion. Her memory was famous, and she could remember vast amounts of detail – all of which was to stand her in good stead. Methodical and resilient, she could always, as she said herself, 'look after her own ship'. She was definitely the boss. Of average height, she was blessed with striking good looks and a beautiful head of curly black hair, and piercing blue eyes that were said to look straight through you. In matters of sailing or business, she could not be fooled. For a formidable businesswoman and sailor, she looked very sweet, which was why she was sometimes called by the pet name Kate Kute.

She was unique. She had a tough start to life, but refused to accept defeat. 'Get everything shipshape,' she always said.

But for all her success, Kate's life was not an easy one.

Her family knew more than their fair share of tragedy – illness robbed Kate of her parents and two of her three sisters within a few short years of each other. She also lived in a time when women were thought of primarily as childbearers, housekeepers and second-class citizens – and certainly a time when women were not expected to run ships and shipping businesses. She was so forward-looking that even when she married, Kate insisted on keeping her own name – unheard-of at the time.

I was completely taken in by the stories. I could tell from my mother what a wonderful woman Kate had been, and many others who knew her told her the same. I was fascinated by her willpower, her determination to succeed in a man's world, her courage in the face of adversity. I knew that she lived in most difficult times. The era during which the *Denbighshire Lass* sailed, from 1857 to 1920, is often looked at with a romantic eye, the time of the Flying Dutchman, the Marie Celeste, Jules Verne's 20,000 Leagues Under the Sea, Mutiny on the Bounty and the South Sea islands. But it was a tough world in which to survive. Some people made vast amounts of wealth through merchant shipping, but for the vast majority, at home and at sea, life was very hard. Many sailors died of hardship and malnutrition.

The whole way of life of those times is now gone. Much of course, is not to be regretted, but this was was also a time when all things were built by hand with no modern tools. The crafts of what was termed the chippie, the carpenter or shipwright, are also gone, and the man who could bend and shape iron for the shipping industry was, as often as not, the same man who shod the horses (the blacksmith or the wrought-iron worker).

It took centuries of refinement for shipbuilders and sailors to master the complex sailing techniques and skills of the big clippers and brigs; it is sad that, by the time these skills had been mastered, and the ships were at their most efficient ever, the sailing ship herself was on the way out, replaced by the steam ships that ploughed the oceans so much faster. Everything else was changing as well – new methods of transport – cars, the internal-combustion engine, steam power, and electricity – became available, and the entire world of industry and manufacture changed beyond recognition. The era of the sailing ship may have been a romantic one, but we must not lose sight of the fact that it was a time of survival, of hardship and of tragedy. The fittest survived – with luck and with some prayers.

I used to love going round the houses as a small boy. At one house, I would knock at the door and, on entering, would be greeted by a shout from the back room of 'Full astern! Full astern!' The voice came from the parrot who was kept there, a bird of the most beautiful colours who had been brought home by my friend's granddad. It was his one cry and he used to repeat it constantly around the house. I always waited for the bird to say something other than 'Full astern!', but he never did.

I would then go down to visit my favourite old lady. It was quite a big house with a lot of big rooms and there seemed to be plenty of cats; black, brown, and more black cats. The house was also crammed with what seemed to me to be everything that could possibly be required on a ship – they were all to be found scattered in various rooms. I would go on some small errand for this lady, who always wore a black shawl and carried rosary beads, and then return to sit by the fire and listen for endless hours to her tales. She was without doubt my favourite storyteller.

Not many boys of twelve or thirteen are lucky enough to have made such a good friend. She was unlike anyone else I knew. She was always alone, it seemed to me, except for the very occasional visit by some relation. But she was a most gentle individual, and someone I'll never forget. She is as clear to me today as the house and the ships' relics and cats which crammed it. I can see them as clearly as if I were back sitting beside her fire, where we would sit watching the bread baking in the open pan. Whatever it was that she had to eat (which was not a whole lot), I was always offered half of it. She also gave me my first-ever comic – she carefully saved for me the colour inserts from American newspapers. They were a very great treat in those days – especially as they were in colour!

Many of this lady's family had been lost at sea, in the Navy or in merchant shipping, or had gone to live in foreign lands, and eventually she had been forced to fend for herself. Years and years later, when she eventually passed away, I was heartbroken at the loss of a very dear friend. I learned a lot from her, not merely about ships and shipping. Like my mother, she also told me about Kate. As I write this, I can smell the bread cooking on her open fire. She told me many stories of how some sailors' wives kept hens and pigs so as to be able to survive when the sailor man of the house was away sailing around Cape Horn or wherever for years at a time. Often people had to eat the food they had kept to feed the poultry with.

Because I was so interested in ships, I saw a painting by an artist named Chappell of the family ship, the *Denbighshire Lass*. I became fascinated with two torpedo-shaped brass objects, kept in the house, which I was told were the ship's speed logs. When you twisted these, a set of dials appeared. They looked as perfect as they must have been on the day they were made.

Though I loved hearing stories about the shipping world and about Kate, I was never really interested in history, either local or worldwide, to any great extent while at school – until I was fortunate to meet with a very learned man who worked with me for many years. He had a deep-rooted fascination with history and this influenced me enormously. I became fascinated listening to him talking abut historical facts and his wide range of knowledge on all subjects. He is someone I will remember always with the greatest gratitude and appreciation. I thank God I had been one of the many who had the company of his wisdom, insight, and great knowledge even for the short time I knew him. Like many more of his friends and acquaintances, I am forever in his debt.

And so the voyage of the *Denbighshire Lass* begins. A voyage not only through all kinds of weather, seas and rivers, but a journey through a time long gone; a time which is indescribable, unforgettable, and thought of with emotion. We see it through rose-coloured glasses as the 'good old days', but perhaps the 'hard old days' would be a better, if less romantic, description.

Chapter 1

THE LAUNCH OF THE *DENBIGHSHIRE LASS*

The year 1857 was a very good one for sea trading. Particularly around the Connah's Quay and north Wales, where there was an abundance of both timber and cheap labour, more and more schooners and brigantines were being launched.

At the end of that July in Flint, north Wales (another great shipbuilding area, where the river Dee flows down from Chester and begins to widen into the sea), shipbuilders were putting the finishing touches to yet another streamlined sixty-two ton schooner, the product of almost four months' work by the master shipwright and his crew. Now, as the crew busily set about completing the masts, jib and main deck, the master inspected the areas of caulking and watched the painter carefully inscribe in gilded old English lettering on the dark-green hull of the schooner the name *Denbighshire Lass*.

The ship was almost completed. The master shipwright's mind went back to the time, only twelve weeks earlier, when only the keel and the skeleton of the ship had stood there. He felt great pride in his team. Every man had worked extremely hard to meet the deadline of the launch date of August 1857.

The *Denbighshire Lass* was sixty-one ton, seventy-two feet four inches by eight feet six inches by nine feet – a graceful and elegant vessel. Her bow was not as sharp as that on a modern ship, which meant that she would need to push a lot of sea in front of her as she moved forward – not perhaps as economical with effort as she might have been. Her stern was rounded.

The *Denbighshire Lass* was owned by James Jones & Co., a company belonging to one of the major shipping families of the Connah's Quay area, and registered to a port of Beaumaris. Her crew at that time included Masters Rolands and J. Cooper, sailing for Jones & Co., and she was listed in the 1863 register as *Denbighshire Lass*, Iron Bolts, Jones & Co. She has been often termed as a Liverpool schooner by merchant seamen, like most of her sister ships at that time sailing the Irish Sea.

Compared to the modern ships, whose synthetic nylon sails are so light and resilient, the *Denbighshire Lass*, like all the other schooners of her time, bore an extraordinary amount of weight for her size: a small schooner, she could be sailed by only two or three men. Even though she, and other schooners like her, were small, it was very hard work handling her sails alone. Yet they could never be ignored; even while the ship was in port, and constantly when she was at sea, the crew had to be aware of the position of the sails, and might have to change the rigging at any moment according to the wind. The hardship of handling such heavy sails, especially when waterlogged, and ropes was a feature of life in those times. The rigging of the ships of the time was extremely complex. The artist Chappell, who painted the first picture I ever saw of the *Denbighshire Lass*, always painted sketched ships from the leeside – that way avoiding the difficult task of depicting such complicated rigging!

The launch of the *Denbighshire Lass* was a great event in Flint. She was to be skippered by a captain from the Connah's Quay district in Wales, for a shipping company which would use her for coasting from Merseyside. The shipwrights and workers, and their families watched the manager and foreman for the signal that sent the schooner gliding into the calm dark water that bitterly cold day in August 1857. She was then christened by one of the managers' wives; and the new sails and rigging were unfolded.

She was ready for her new life.

For the next twenty-nine years, the *Denbighshire Lass* would pursue the tramp trade, as it was called: journeying with one cargo in the hope of picking up another on arrival at the original destination. Her port of register, Beaumaris, was not far from her original launching place at the river Dee, and that of Connah's Quay was well established and had many shipping companies and insurance firms. The *Denbighshire Lass* made considerable voyages in this area. From my researches in the Accounts and Voyages National Archives, it appears that she sailed from Beaumaris to Liverpool, then to Carrickfergus, Belfast (and frequently as far north as Derry) and Glasgow, returning to the river Dee and Connah's Quay to begin a completely new voyage. This brutal circuit would continue month after month until winter arrived, when she would lie in port. Her cargo could consist of anything, from bricks and tiles to slate or textiles. She would also trade to Swansea and areas of the Bristol Channel.

The 1860s and 70s were the days of the sailing craft, and there was always a forest of masts to be seen in any port. Trade around Beaumaris, Connah's Quay, Birkenhead, Liverpool, Shotton and Garston was flourishing. But by the same token, there were plenty of schooners ready to take on the work, so competition was extremely keen and a reliable, seaworthy, fast-sailing and well-manned ship was a must. It was not until the 1880s that steamships would appear in any great numbers.

During this time, many shipping firms had fleets of similar schooners and, because of the ever-increasing market and demand for transport spawned by the Industrial Revolution, ships were bought and sold frequently between companies hoping for a bigger share of business. This probably explains why, in 1868, the *Denbighshire Lass* was sold to Frances and James Bowers Chester, who in turn auctioned her back, in 1871, to her original owners, Jones & Co. Large repairs had been carried out on the ship during the years 1867-1871, and the Bowers Chesters needed to get some of their money back.

By 1871, however, she was fully refurbished and once more seaworthy, and was back again on the tramp trade, voyaging from her home port of Beaumaris as far south as Cornwall.

Again her crew included Masters Rolands and J. Cooper. This was not at all unusual – many sailors become strongly attached to their ship: 'We always look after our ship because she always looks after us.' Ship and crew can become one in the relentlessness of the work necessary to keep the vessel shipshape. The life of the crew is inextricably tied up with the ship.

This time the *Denbighshire Lass* was to remain with Jones & Co. for many years; after her 1867 repairs she must have been in as good condition as the day she was launched. It is a mark of the craftsmanship of the shipwrights, working with what today appear primitive tools, that after twenty-one years' hard sailing, she was as robust as ever.

At that time, there were two highly influential shipping families in Connah's Quay: the Coppacks, who were involved in all aspects of merchant shipping, and the Reneys, who owned large numbers of ships, which it appears they also managed, and who also looked after other aspects of the shipping business, including insurance and repairs. It was not surprising, then, that the Reney family would be one of the purchasers of the *Denbighshire Lass*, and in 1880, she was sold to them. The family also set up the Dee Shipowners' Mutual Insurance Association at about the same time.

According to the National Archives account of Voyage and Crews, the *Denbighshire Lass* would now be sailed by John Edwards (born 1855) of Amlioch, William Edwards (born 1828), and John Flanagan (born 1846). The skipper and crew had worked for the Reney family for many a long year. The schooner would once again continue her tramp trade to Belfast, Liverpool and Connah's Quay – no business could be turned down. Tied to such a huge company as the Reney family's, the *Denbighshire Lass* would not be idle long.

The *Denbighshire Lass* must have been an extremely sturdy craft to survive those voyages. But in 1886, she was purchased and brought to Arklow, Co. Wicklow, by Edward and Elizabeth Tyrrell, who had been involved with the coasting trade.

Chapter 2

LIFE ON BOARD SHIP

In the nineteenth century, any young man who, through necessity – and poverty and the Famine forced many to sea – decided that he would go seafaring, would firstly join a local vessel like the *Denbighshire Lass*, and then, after learning the rudiments, would go on foreign trips on the clippers. There was fishing around Arklow, but there was no money in that, it was said. A sailor on one of those clippers, or on a three-masted barque which might sail to Chile or even more exotic locations, would earn as much in a week as he would make with six months' work on a local coaster such as the *Denbighshire Lass*. The motivation to go to 'deep sea', as it was called, was very strong.

And before any of these giant sailing craft would take their final encounter around Cape Hope, the policy was to take on extra men, as all hands knew that if any bad weather was encountered, some sailors could be lost around the Cape.

This sometimes happened when the sails were frozen up. Upon being unfolded, they would unfurl very quickly, tossing the poor unfortunate seaman overboard in the most miserable weather conditions. It really was only the fittest who survived. But this was the price that was known to be paid.

I have been told of Arklow seamen sailing in ships like 3,700-ton barques, brigantines and clippers with patent fuel (a form of briquettes), to Chile and around Cape Hope.

Some of the brigantines had a speed of twelve to fourteen knots – i.e. full sea speed. The voyage from Port Talbot around the Cape, on a ship like the *James Kerr*, owned by William Thomas of Liverpool, took 134 days, all being well. On board there were sixteen sailors and eight apprentices: a huge volume of manpower, as well as sailpower, was required to keep the giant ships moving.

When these huge ships arrived in Chile, there were no harbours as such at which they could discharge their cargoes, just a never-ending bank of sand. So all of the cargoes were manhandled from the main ship to smaller craft for off-loading, and this was time-consuming, back-breaking work.

Most of the steering on these ships was carried out by the sails. Some sailors at that time went to Australia on three-masted barques and clippers, on leaving Liverpool. It would take eighty-six days to get to Sydney.

The design and construction of smaller ships, similar to the *Denbighshire Lass* left a lot to be desired. The hull shape, height of the masts, the measurements between bow and stern compared with those of port to starboard side; plus the possibility of waterlogged sails, made these craft very unstable in poor weather, even with ballast (cargo); and they were not really designed for any great speed. On several occasions the *Denbighshire Lass* herself was almost lost in storms and gale-force winds. Two years after the *Denbighshire Lass* was launched in 1859, one of the worst storms ever recorded caused a catastrophe of gigantic proportions, resulting in some 300 lives lost and over 100 ships sunk around Britain alone. Another such voyage was when she left the port of Swansea in 1897, heading for the Irish coastline. Heavy wind and rain came on without warning, to the degree that the cargo, some of which was coal, shifted and the ship began listing to the port side. Combined with the almost unmanageably water-logged sails, this made progress difficult and highly dangerous – any listing ship would take in a great deal of water into the cargo area regardless of whether it was battened down or not. As luck would have it, the vessel accidentally righted itself; the cargo shifting once more to midship position and the small storm which had erupted so quickly abated in like manner. But, in some of these encounters, the *Denbighshire Lass* and her crew would face mountainous waves in a stretch of sea that would be most inhospitable and life-threatening.

The crew of any craft depending on sail power would have to be ready to react at all times to any changes in the weather; waves would also manipulate the bow movement.

Some old papers discovered in the 1950s include notes written by Kate to her husband John regarding the damage caused by such heavy weather during a voyage of the *Denbighshire Lass*. After listing the vital repairs to be carried out, she commented on how lucky they all had been to survive this ordeal in the Bristol Channel. The final line, in Kate's copperplate writing, reads: 'Always seek understanding in He who is the truth – God.'

Repairs

Every family operating these vessels, like Kate and later, her husband (skipper John Fitzpatrick), had to ensure that all was right; their very existence depended on their ship.

Hence the never-ending work of keeping everything ship-shape.

One of the main jobs was the mending of sails. The sails on a ship such as the *Denbighshire Lass* were extremely heavy, as they were made from an extremely heavy-duty canvas; if they became waterlogged, the weight was enormous. When they became damp, therefore, as they frequently did, they required a lot of manpower to move them. If a sail became damaged it had to be repaired immediately; otherwise the wind would destroy it entirely, putting the whole ship at risk.

Repairs to the sails were sometimes carried out on deck using a type of stitch that's called a herring-bone: i.e., a crisscross stitch in the shape of an 'X'. The torn sail was repaired with powdered hemp twine threaded through a large needle. Mending sails was a painstaking exercise, but a very necessary one; even the tiniest tear could lengthen in storms and cause disaster. Every member of the *Denbighshire Lass*'s crew, including Kate herself, was capable of turning their hand to this essential task. The person who repaired the sails would also occasionally be expected to stitch up the gash on a gaping wound with sailmaking twine disinfected in some form of spirit such as whiskey or other alcohol, until the patient could be brought ashore.

Apart from mending the sails, the ship's crew also carried out other minor repairs, such as some timber repair.

The deck would be continually cleaned with a mop and water. Tar was applied on some parts of the ship to keep out water; its application was a full-time job and was accepted as part of normal duties.

While there was no dock in Arklow at this time – and would not be until 1910, although it was a busy port with many ships from Norway and Britain – some schooners and ketches were given minor repairs to their hull side by the following method: with the use of pulley blocks from the shore, the vessel was put into shallow water, then heaved sideways by the blocks until the boat was partially capsized. The ship would be left that way until repairs were made, after which she would be uprighted again. The *Denbighshire Lass* would also pick up cargoes of coal at Garston. At any one of Garston's three docks, it was a common sight to see a vessel pulled sideways until she was listed enough to have full repairs carried out.

Even during the winter months, when the *Denbighshire Lass* would not be sailing, there was always an endless list of repairs to sails and rigging, applying coats of pitch and tar, replacing dead eyes on the rigging, timber repairs, and cleaning. It was a never-ending round of chores which was necessary to ensure the safety of the crew and the valuable cargoes.

The work on board ship, therefore, was back-breaking, dangerous and demanding, yet conditions were also bad. The stories of sailors on the larger ships at this time, right up until 1905, tell of rotten food on board, which naturally led to scurvy among the crew. Food was scarce and rarely appealing: when sailors who sailed on large clippers on rations of food were told that word had come from the people controlling the rations that the margarine ration was increased from two ounces to half a pound, there would be a mini celebration – it meant that they could cook in margarine. Food was always difficult to obtain – hence sailors would try to catch rabbits and pheasants when the ship was docked. Those who sailed to places like Rio maintained that you could acquire just about any commodity in return for a bar of soap.

The ship's stove was lit in the morning but would be put out at midday to conserve fuel – therefore sailors had to keep warm by other means, even in the roughest of weathers.

Hardly surprising, then, that sailors, even if they survived dangerous storms and high seas, often fell prey to illness. In very hot weather the men were obliged to eat salt, as this replaced valuable minerals they lost while sweating and prevented severe and crippling cramps and more. There were all kinds of sicknesses on board these ships. Apart from tropical ones like yellow fever, or nutritional scurvy, sea boils were a particularly unpleasant scourge, caused by a deficiency in the diet. Ideally they were overcome by the sailor staying in his bunk for almost a week and drinking water; however, as often as not, the water was not clean and it was necessary to drink rum or other liquids, all of which were probably not very good for a sick man!

Although sailors were noted for their taste for strong drink, it was not uncommon to see some crew members on any merchant ship sporting a badge called the Father Matthew badge, which was the forerunner to the now well-known Pioneer pin. This Father Matthew badge was the sign of a teetotaller. Kate, a non-drinker herself, disapproved of alcohol; one of her strictest rules was that no one was allowed on board the *Denbighshire Lass* if they had drink taken. The crew were careful of the grog when Kate was around.

Sanitation on board ships such as these small schooners was primitive in the extreme; there were no real toilet facilities as such, only a type of removable bucket, the contents of which would be heaved over the side.

The seafaring profession, like any other, has its superstitions, fears, folklore, beliefs – and facts. But the wide-open sea, even to the most experienced sailors, can be the most inhospitable and frightening place on earth. Perhaps superstitions such as not allowing a whistling woman on board helped them to cope. Sailors would put their trust in the protection of the Lord and read passages from the

Bible daily. Even now there is always a Bible on board every ship, and its presence can prove comforting in a world where unpredictable weather can create tidal waves, storms and more.

Anyone who was at sea for a long period of time tended to feel very much out of touch with what was happening in their home place, and thus sailors, then and now, tend often to live in their own world, staying even longer on board ship. In effect, mariners led two different lives. Sometimes it must have seemed impossible to leave one world and enter another, leaving one's family and home behind.

Given that conditions were so harsh, it was not surprising that when a craft was docked somewhere like New York or Sydney, many men jumped ship to find a better life – and who could blame them?

Chapter 3

THE TYRRELLS

The years 1875 to 1888 would bring enormous changes to a young woman, Kate Tyrrell, and her family, who lived in Arklow, Co. Wicklow.

The town, like many others in Ireland, had lost many people to the emigration forced on the land by the Great Famine, but now, almost twenty years after that great calamity, the local community was beginning to gather itself together again and reform, while the Irish nation was going through the most traumatic period of its history. Despite the fact that hunger no longer threatened, conditions were still dreadful. The fortunate ones were those with a roof over their head, clothes for their backs and some food for their bellies – but even so people were still dying young and infant mortality was high.

The blacksmith was a man most in demand at the time, not just for his work in shoeing horses, but because he was required for the wrought-iron repairs to the ships' implements. Many of the men in the town, however, were forced to become sailors, with the result that the women were left to carry on as best they could. These hard-working women are to be remembered with great affection, dressed as they were in the traditional shawls under which they seemed to carry almost everything they owned. They led hard lives, and lonely ones: they had to look after their families alone, often for years at a time. Making ends meet was never easy. They were, after all, living in an era when mortality was very high, when the vast majority of people were underfed and underclothed, and when many, many people died young of consumption, rickets and many other preventable diseases. A book known as the 'Carysfort Book on Arklow' contains most informative pictures of the houses in the town during the *Denbighshire Lass* years. The only houses in Arklow that were not included in that huge book were dwellings deemed as 'freehold'. All hand-painted, the illustrations show people standing by their thatched cottages, the men smoking clay pipes, the women wrapped in shawls. There are pigs around some of the houses. The book is now being copied for posterity. It is an important volume and deserves to be preserved.

Most of Arklow's houses at the time were thatched cottages, though there were a few with slate roofs. Kate and her family, however, were privileged in comparison to many of the people in Arklow. Edward Tyrrell, her father, was a mariner and owned several schooners, which he also sailed as master, employing others as required to sail his other ships. He was also an astute businessman. They lived near a prosperous area of King's Hill, close to many of the houses of seafaring families. A shop near Meadows Lane was also connected to the maritime life for many years.

Edward and his wife Elizabeth had four daughters. Ellen was born in 1861, and in 1863, as far as I can ascertain (she was always reticent about her age), was followed by Kate. Ellen had dark brown hair and was a relaxed, easy-going child, unlike Kate, who could be abrupt and who had a fiery personality. The third daughter was Alecia, who was born in 1867, and Lucy, born in 1868. Alecia was very like Kate, while Lucy was very much her father's daughter and would turn out to be the tallest of the four sisters.

The bond between all four girls was very strong, despite their differences. They had, after all, grown up as we have seen, in a world where survival was paramount, where, only a few years before, the country had been ravaged by famine. It was a world which left its mark on these young girls.

Kate, growing up at this time, would have seen cartoons of Queen Victoria, surrounded by all the peoples of the British Empire as if by children, while the ungrateful child that was Ireland stood apart. The visions of Thomas Davis and Wolfe Tone had not materialised. Daniel O'Connell's work seemed to have come to nothing.

Kate's mother Elizabeth was very strict with her daughters, and Kate always made certain she was immaculately dressed going to and from school. There were, of course, no cosmetics as we know them for the young women of Kate's day, but girls would make use of many traditional treatments: goat's-milk baths and the washing of one's face with buttermilk to keep wrinkles away, along with the use of olive oil for almost everything, including rheumatic pains and God knows what. Kate always appeared slim and energetic – possibly because of the wasplike waists which were the fashion of the time and which must have been an enormous restriction on a woman of her undoubted energy and vitality.

But though she had her mother's looks, Kate had all her father's mannerisms, no doubt absorbed during the many hours she spent with him on his ship. As the children grew up, it became clear that Kate was the one who would follow in her father's footsteps. Her older sister Ellen was close to their mother, but Kate was always more attached to their father, and no doubt this was what helped develop her forceful personality: though Ellen was the older of the two, there was no doubt as to who was the leader.

Her sisters showed little interest in their father's business, but Kate was always eager for ships, and immersed herself in the maritime world from her earliest childhood. She spent many hours on board ship familiarising herself with ship charts and navigational equipment. She found a keen teacher in her father, and would listen with great attention to all that was said. By the time Kate was ten years old, she already had a wealth of knowledge about seafaring, gathered during the endless hours she spent after school on the quayside and on board her father's schooners, especially when one was moored in the Arklow river, Inbhear Mor. By the age of twelve she could write up shipping-journal entries and records. Seafaring became second nature to her, just as it was to her father.

By the time she was fifteen years of age, and a strikingly beautiful young woman, Kate had, therefore, done a considerable amount of sailing and was familiar with many sailing and navigational techniques. She would also help with the family business and with keeping the shipping records, though her long hours down at the harbour did not hinder her formal education. She and her sister Ellen were always top of their class in school, where she learned bookkeeping and business studies, both of which were to come in very useful when she was required to help with the family business papers. In such times people naturally looked to see who would take over the running of the family, or the family business, should the main breadwinner die. Perhaps Edward Tyrrell, as a man of his times, would have liked a son to carry on the business; in any case it seemed inevitable that it would be Kate who would follow in his footsteps. He began to groom her to replace him, and Kate was more than willing to learn.

Edward Tyrrell had close associates in the shipping of vessels to and from Arklow. Among these was the Brennan family, who lived in an area of Arklow, now named Bridge Street, where there were cottages near Sweeps Corner – a place that derived its name from the chimney sweeps who could be found there. Laurence and his own family all hailed from Co. Wexford, and originally lived in an area called Moneygarrow, Inch, Gorey, Co. Wexford, but he moved into Arklow when he married. Laurence's sister Ann was the mother of John and Thomas Fitzpatrick, two men who would become very close to the Tyrrells.

Laurence Brennan had four children, all of whom lived in Arklow: Jim, Pat, Sam and daughter Annie. He had on numerous occasions made voyages for Edward Tyrrell, and this family were always close associates of the Tyrrells. His sons learned much from him and were also to become seamen of renown; he would sail with them on many voyages. Jim Brennan became a nautical instructor whom many mariners would visit for training; he was later to move to Meadow's Lane in Arklow. Pat Brennan, to whom I often spoke, was a delight. His stories of his travels around the globe were breathtaking. When he married, he moved to Cron Cribín, Inch, Gorey, Co. Wexford. This most impressive man lived to be a hundred years old. Wexford people are so helpful and full of camaraderie, and they hold strong allegiances to their home county. This is possibly the reason that Laurence's son Pat moved back to near his own home place when he married after travelling so much during a life of seafaring. He took to farming as eagerly as he had taken to the seas, and mastered this craft as well. Pat Brennan was the only sailor of whom I have ever heard it said that 'This man ploughed the seas and ploughed the land both successfully'.

Kate and the Brennans would become very close shipping associates, and even at the age of seventeen or eighteen, she would often join them aboard ship to sail to Connah's Quay.

In 1882 Kate Tyrrell was nineteen years old, with her eyes on a bright future in the man's world of shipping. She could not have known of the hard blows that were about to fall.

Chapter 4

TRAGEDY

In April 1882, when Kate returned from a voyage to Connah's Quay with her father and Laurence Brennan, she learned that her fifteen-year-old sister Alecia had been very ill for some time and that her health was failing rapidly. The scourge of the time, consumption, had struck her as it had so many others.

In May Alecia became acutely ill and died.

Her death affected Kate badly. Her world crumbled around her. Kate's faith was strong, but it was a major blow to watch her sister fight to hold on to life for months, only to be taken in the end by consumption. The doctor said that Alecia had had a fever, and that he had done everything he could, but now the funeral arrangements had to be made.

Edward Tyrrell handled this, as Elizabeth had taken her daughter's death very badly and her husband had great difficulty consoling her.

At this time, it was rare for every town to have an undertaker; this service was carried out by people in the community. Although Arklow did have a firm of undertakers called Bradford, living where the roundabout now is, a family living near the Tyrrells who came to do this sad task for them. They laid out the body and arranged the wake for the beautiful fifteen-year-old girl, so very like Kate, who had been taken away so tragically early. This tradition, of the laying-out of the body by friends rather than professionals, made the funeral far more personal than it can be nowadays when matters are looked after by undertakers – kind, competent, caring no doubt, but not part of the family.

Alecia's funeral took place on 29 May, 1882. Alecia's remains were brought to the church by horse-drawn hearse. Edward and his wife Elizabeth, with their three remaining daughters, said the prayers with the congregation. The mourners included Laurence Brennan.

The Tyrrells knew, of course, that such a tragically early death was no rare occurence in the difficult times in which they lived. But that was no consolation to the family who walked, shattered, from the graveyard.

The death of Alecia left an indelible mark on Kate, but she kept up her objectives of moving forward and looking to the future. She was an inspiration to her sisters Ellen and Lucy, though Kate herself was under much pressure, as Elizabeth, her mother, had become very ill after Alecia's death. Kate was forced to take on an enormous burden for such a young girl.

Because of her mother's illness, Kate had to take over the task of keeping the books for Edward's ships, something her mother had been used to doing. But the young woman's indomitable nature rose to the task of looking after her sisters, comforting her sick mother, and carrying out the bookkeeping for the schooners under her father's control.

However, Elizabeth did not recover; indeed, her illness

became so acute that Edward decided to remain at home, rather than spending his time away in the harsh and demanding world of the tramp trade, and Laurence Brennan and his crew took over the sailing of his ships.

During 1882 Laurence Brennan's nephew, John Fitzpatrick from Ballycanew (the son of his sister Ann), joined Laurence on board Edward's schooner. Five foot seven and with a fine moustache, John was sometimes called Parks or Johnny Patrick – the name Parks, I'm told, came from his easygoing personality. He was to sail many a voyage for Edward Tyrrell. Just as the Brennans had, John also became great friends with Kate's family, and was a great support to them in their difficult times.

John had two brothers, Moses and Tom, and two sisters, Julia and Mary. Both Moses and Tom Brennan were great seamen, although Moses preferred foreign trips while John liked coasting. Tom was the quiet one, and the tallest of the three brothers; like John, both he and Moses sported fashionable moustaches.

Around 1882, John Fitzpatrick was well aware that his own family were starting to leave the home place. Ballycanew was a farming area, but, like everywhere else at the time, its small farms could not provide a living for whole families, and many of its people were forced to eke out a living some other way. The menfolk usually ended up emigrating or seafaring. There was precious little else for them to do. Mary Fitzpatrick had already emigrated to England and was living in Liverpool. Moses was spending more and more time away on foreign voyages and sea trips, and there was talk of him emigrating for good. Julia and Tom had both left to live in Arklow. Tom had married and lived in an area called Cox Corner, in Tinahask; and Julia married a man called Greene, and lived at the top of the town, near Saint Saviour's Church.

At the age of nineteen and in the absence of her father,

Kate Tyrrell was now the head of the Tyrrell family. Edward Tyrrell relied on her to look after the other women and to keep the business going. In fact Edward depended on his daughter Kate for a great deal, especially when, that October of 1882, Elizabeth's sickness reached crisis point. Elizabeth's health deteriorated until, on 12 December 1882, at the age of forty-four, she died of the consumption that had so cruelly taken her daughter only a few months before.

Yet again, Kate and her family had to bury one of their own. With Kate's assistance, Edward once again made the funeral arrangements. The bleak December weather meant that it was freezing cold. There was a heavy blanket of snow on the ground, and the horse-drawn hearse bearing the body of Elizabeth Tyrrell moved slowly and heavily, the horse's breath hanging frozen in the still air.

At the graveyard the prayers were read while the earth that had been removed to make room for the coffin froze under the snow and the ice.

Her sister and her beloved mother had died within six months of each other, but Kate – still only nineteen years of age – was not allowed time to mourn. Soon after her mother's funeral she was once again left in charge of the Tyrrell business while her father and Laurence Brennan again sailed the family ships.

She had experienced great tragedy, but Kate never dwelt on insurmountable problems. Her father had once promised her – his daughter who loved sailing as he did – that one day she would own her own ship. This was the one thing that Kate looked forward to; perhaps it gave her strength to continue when despair must have threatened to take her over.

By 1885, Kate was twenty-two years old and a mother figure to her sisters Lucy and Ellen, who looked to her for guidance. Already this extraordinary young woman was wise in worldly matters. Together she and Ellen looked after the house and the business. Lucy was still going to school, but she was very frail, far more so than either of her two remaining sisters. She suffered a great deal of sickness and was often forced to remain in bed for weeks at a time, looked after by Kate and Ellen. God only knows how they must have feared another loss.

The years 1885 and 1886 were to prove to be testing ones for these three young women.

The Tyrrell family, touched by tragedy as they had already been, were plagued with sickness and ill health. Edward Tyrrell had suffered heart trouble from time to time, but it never stopped him sailing his ships on the brutally demanding tramp trade to Connah's Quay, Garston or Liverpool, and thence home again with cargo to Dublin, Waterford and Courtown. This formidable spirit he passed on to his daughter. These trips could be quite brief – two or three weeks at most – and he would look forward to arriving into his home dock, where he would be greeted by Kate and Ellen, and occasionally, although not often because of her illness, by his youngest surviving daughter Lucy.

The Brennan family and the Tyrrells were still very close; the Brennans were an enormous support to Kate. Kate often accompanied her father on his voyages, and when this happened, Laurence Brennan's wife would take care of Ellen and Lucy.

Then, on one occasion in 1885, Edward Tyrrell asked his daughter Kate to accompany him, and the faithful Laurence Brennan, to Connah's Quay to inspect a ship with him.

Chapter 5

THE PURCHASE OF THE
DENBIGHSHIRE LASS

Edward had wanted to acquire a new ship for some time, and had finalised a deal to sell two of his old schooners, bringing him the money he needed to buy a new one. Kate, closely involved as she was in the business, was very excited by the idea. Edward had already made arrangements for the ship he would like to buy, and now he was bringing her to Connah's Quay to see her for herself.

On their arrival at Connah's Quay, Kate and Edward made their way up the river Dee to an area very near Flint, and it was there, in a berth on the quayside, that Kate Tyrrell first saw the *Denbighshire Lass*. She could see from the size of the sails, even at midship position, that this was a much bigger vessel that the one in which they had sailed to England. She was immediately impressed by the schooner, and as soon as they could, they boarded the *Denbighshire Lass*.

Kate was overwhelmed with this coaster, which she knew had been owned by the renowned Reney family. It was her first time setting foot on the *Denbighshire Lass*, yet instinctively Kate seemed to know exactly where everything was kept, even in the skipper's cabin. It must have been a sight in those days to see such a small and pretty young woman as Kate Kute, as she was known, strutting around the deck like a man, examining everything expertly, casting her experienced eye over every part of the ship, completely at home in this masculine environment.

After examining the deck and observing that the *Denbighshire Lass* was in very good condition and had been well painted up (the 'gold' 'Olde Englishe' lettering of the ship's name stood out very well), Kate was beside herself with excitement. It was late in the evening on an autumn's day, yet the air was warm and the river Dee calm. Kate could see port and starboard diaptrix lights shining red and green, and the kerosene lamps. She and her father turned to descend into the skipper's cabin at the ship's stern.

'Kate,' her father told her, 'this is your ship, and she's going to be registered in your name.'

It was the fulfilment of all Kate's hopes and dreams – the dreams she had had since she was a very young girl. Now they were all coming to pass.

Entering the cabin, Kate could see the brass ship's speed logs on the table beside the charts, and some legal documents in a folder neatly labelled *Denbighshire Lass*.

She was overwhelmed with the ship – how new it was compared with her father's two old schooners, and how well kept and well maintained. She asked about the involvement of her sisters in all matters concerning this wonderful ship. Her father told her that they would all have an equal share in the ship, but that if anything were to happen to him, the *Denbighshire Lass* would be Kate's responsibility. This did nothing to still her excitement, especially when she thought that she and her father would soon be sailing this beautiful schooner back to Ireland.

To finalise all the business and paperwork involved in the purchase of the ship, Kate, Edward and Laurence Brennan stayed until the next day. Business concluded, they finally set sail for home in their new schooner, the *Denbighshire Lass*. Kate, her usual mariner self, was looking at the charts and examining the speed logs when they were hauled off in the drawline.

They had good sailing weather for the journey – there was plenty of wind and it was quite warm. Because Edward's heart complaint demanded that he take things easy on board, Laurence Brennan took charge of the wheel. Standing by him, Kate was intrigued. After all, this was now her ship. For the first time in her life, Kate attempted to control the ship at the wheel and was successful.

While this was referred to as 'taking the wheel', in actual fact the 'wheel' on smaller craft such as the *Denbighshire Lass* was really called a 'tiller'. The tiller was a handle or boom which in turn was attached to the rudder. On a ship the size of the *Denbighshire Lass*, the tiller was moved with the aid of ropes through 'dead eyes'. These were wooden blocks with holes for tightening the ropes. With a large sail and full wind, using these to manoeuvre the craft took enormous strength. As the tiller was moved left or right, the ship moved accordingly. The tiller had some advantages over the wheel system, mainly that the ship reacted much faster and was thus far more manoeuvrable. With one push of the tiller, the craft could immediately respond, turning left or right as needed, while many complete turns of the wheel were needed to accomplish a similar operation on a larger ship.

Sometimes the sailor in control of the tiller would be adjusting the sails at the same time. Enormous discipline was required as the work was physically hard and demanding.

Although Laurence had seen Kate on board ship before, he was now extremely impressed with this young female mariner who was able to dictate tacking methods and navigation course settings as well or better than any man. He told Edward that she was better than most sailors he knew.

'I've always known that,' was Edward's reply.

The excitement of the voyage was enough to rob Kate of all sleep, and she was happy enough to take the tiller more often as they headed for the Wicklow coastline en route to Arklow. But there was one port of call first. The *Denbighshire Lass* was to sail to Dublin where she would be registered, and where she would pick up a cargo of tiles for the Arklow area. This took six hours, but then they were back on course for home. Again Kate proved how physically robust she was for a slight young woman as she turned the wheel and navigated as competently as any sailor.

They moored in the river estuary at Arklow, to be greeted by Ellen and Lucy, who had come to the quayside with Laurence's wife and sons. All were thrilled at the new vessel and how well she looked.

After the *Denbighshire Lass* had been inspected by all hands, the Tyrrells and the Brennans made their way home.

They were very proud of their new acquisition.

Chapter 6

MORE TRAGEDY

Kate was very excited and happy. Her father had accomplished the purchase of the new family ship in her name, although the official papers said that her sisters Ellen and Lucy had an equal share in the *Denbighshire Lass*. This was normal procedure in an age when few people lived beyond forty-five. It ensured that one young member of the family – in this case Kate – was always motivated to take care of the business and that there was always somebody to take over should the worst happen. No one would want to see a family business built up over possibly generations of hard work pass into the hands of strangers.

The *Denbighshire Lass* had a very busy year in 1885, and was sailed by Laurence Brennan with a crew of three sailors – mate, able seaman and boy. So busy was the tramp trade that Edward himself also skippered the vessel on occasion.

A typical account of a voyage in 1885 (1885 list of Accounts of Voyages and Crew, National Archives) reads as follows:

Laying up at Connah's Quay 1st January – 14th February
Left 20 February, arrive Belfast 24th February
Left Belfast 1st March, arrive Duddon 3rd March
Left 20th March, arrive Connah's Quay 6th March
Left 13th April, arrive Carrickfergus 16th April
Left 20th April, arrive Cork 28th April
Left 18th May, arrive Barrow 1st June
Left 9th June, arrive Liverpool 5th July.

Signed: John Edwards
Master, *Denbighshire Lass*
(at Liverpool) July 1885.

Kate spent any free time she had on board ship. As Edward's heart problem was becoming more and more acute, he now left a lot of the actual sailing to Laurence Brennan and began to take life at a slower pace, though he did, from time to time, sail the *Denbighshire Lass* himself. Between them, Edward and Kate looked after all the book-keeping and administration associated with shipping – cargo manifests, voyages, insurance, port dues and so on. But in the early part of 1886, Edward suggested that Kate should sail with Laurence to Connah's Quay and the Bristol Channel. Kate, of course, was delighted with this. Edward allowed her to do much of the navigation and course charting, and also to help with the sails, the rigging and the steering. While, as we have seen, controlling the wheel was a demanding task, Kate had already proved herself more than up to it.

In early 1886, Kate was to voyage with Laurence Brennan to Cumberland Basin. On returning to Arklow, her father then took on a new crew and sailed to Cardiff to relieve Laurence. The list of voyages and crew for this time reads as follows:

Edward Tyrrell – Managing Owner

Crew	Year of Birth	Capacity
Edward Tyrrell	1833	Master
Charles Brown	1856	Mate
Patrick Farrell	1866	AB
Michael Kearon	1868	Boy

Voyage for 7th July 1886 in *Denbighshire Lass* by Edward Tyrrell.

From Cardiff 12th January 1886, arrive Wexford 25th January 1886
Left 22nd March 1886, arrive Garston 24th March 1886
Left 11th April 1886, arrive Greystones 12th April 1886
Left 8th May 1886, arrive West Bank 18th May 1886
Left 22nd May 1886, arrive Dublin 26th May 1886
Left 13th June 1886, arrive Garston 20th June 1886
Remain in Garston 1886.

Signed: Edward Tyrrell – 7th July 1886.

During this long voyage, Edward's heart complaint worsened to such a degree that he could no longer move from the ship. His health deteriorated rapidly and, on 7th July 1886, the very day he signed the above voyage sheet, Edward Tyrrell died at Garston on board the *Denbighshire Lass*.

Kate was at home in Arklow when the news of the death of her beloved father reached her. Now truly head of the family, she had no time to grieve, for she had much to do. First she had to organise Laurence Brennan and a new crew to go to Garston to bring back the *Denbighshire Lass* and the body of her father.

On returning to Arklow, Laurence Brennan and Kate's friend John Fitzpatrick moored the *Denbighshire Lass* once again in the river, and the coffined body of skipper Edward Tyrrell was taken from ship to shore and placed in a horse-drawn hearse. This time Kate took care of the funeral arrangements, helped by Edward's friend Michael O'Toole, and had to tear herself away from her private sorrow to choose a coffin for her father. One can only imagine the pain this tragedy caused her and her two remaining sisters. Kate and Ellen, twenty-five and twenty-seven years old, faced the responsibility of looking after Lucy and the family business without a mother or a father.

After the funeral details were finalised, Kate had to decide what was best for the family. The *Denbighshire Lass* had been owned by Edward but now was entirely Kate's. Kate was aware that her name, as a woman's, would not be allowed on much of the official shipping paperwork, or in many of the registers. As managing owner of the ship, Kate took the decision to let Laurence Brennan put his name down as owner, but she determined that she would not rest until every piece of paper relating to the *Denbighshire Lass* named her as owner.

It would take her until 1914.

Kate had always been close to her father; closer than any of her sisters had been. Yet as head of the family, she could not allow her feelings to show. She had no time to mourn as she must have wished. She, Ellen and Lucy had to fend for themselves.

Kate had to look after the family business as well as the shipping paperwork. As a shipowner and a business-woman, Kate was invading a very masculine world. But she made up her mind that no obstacle was going to stop her.

By 1888 Kate appeared to have recovered from the tragedy of her father's death aboard her beloved ship, and to have reorganised her life, her family and her business.

The shipping industry was doing as well as could be expected and under her more than competent leadership the family business thrived. She made sure that the *Denbighshire Lass* was constantly on the seas: her main routes now covered coasting to Cork, Dungarvan and Liverpool with various different cargoes.

But during November and December of that year, when the *Denbighshire Lass* was laid up in port, tragedy was yet again to strike Kate's life.

Never strong, Kate's younger sister Lucy became seriously ill and began to display the symptoms of the consumption which had killed her mother and her sister Alecia. One can only imagine the dread that this caused for the two sisters who had already seen so much tragedy in their young lives.

On 17 November 1888, two years after her father had died at the age of fifty-six, Lucy Tyrrell died at the tender age of twenty.

As the playwright Eugene O'Neill has stated, 'There is no future, it's just the past happening over and over again now'. Once again, Kate was left to handle the funeral arrangements, but this time she did so completely alone. Ellen did nothing to help, being more than willing to place the entire responsibility on the shoulders of her more competent sister. The stress must have been intolerable, but Kate showed real signs of strain only once. Before the funeral, when Kate could not reach the priest, she became so angry that she swore she'd call the Protestant minister instead, shocking many of the pious people around her. Her external attitude made her appear to many to be as hard as steel, but a great load had fallen on her young shoulders when her mother had died, and since the death of her father it seemed that she had to carry it entirely alone. Her inner resources carried her through, but at times she was extremely lonely.

As Lucy was placed beside her parents and her sister in the cold grave, Kate stood with Ellen and Laurence Brennan at the graveside and swore that she would not be defeated. She would make the company a success.

Kate Tyrrell always looked forward. It was her great strength, and it may have been what saved her. Her losses might have broken a weaker woman, but for her, life went on. She put all her considerable resources, physical, mental and financial, into the family business. As members of families die, connections are broken with others. But Kate felt that she must now start to rebuild.

Chapter 7

A WORKING SHIP:
1888 – 1900

As she and Ellen attempted to pick up the pieces and come to terms with their shocking bereavement, it took a long time for Kate to come to terms with the recent tragedies in her life, particularly the death of her father to whom she had been so close and from whom she had learned so much.

Her response was to become businesslike and well organised. She threw herself into her work. She made frequent journeys on shipping affairs. She missed Edward's advice and guidance sorely, but would not let that stop her; whenever she needed some advice on the financial aspects of running the company, she would usually find the answer in one of the books she studied incessantly.

She believed in being accountable for what she did and so made it a point to be familiar with all the technicalities of paperwork and documents. Some port authorities were sticklers for sailing details, but Kate would prove she was right and quite often stood her ground to get her way and would, if necessary, substantiate her claims with paperwork.

Her handwriting was like her appearance. It was well groomed and very legible, and she was meticulous about all aspects of her letter writing. She made some studies of people's handwriting and often made remarks saying that 'they never dot their letter 'i's' and that 'this had a meaning'. She had a sharp knowledge of characteristic handwriting meanings and would sum up very quickly a person's main character points from their handwriting. She was very seldom incorrect in her deductions on this.

Like everything she was involved in, she learned the shipping business inside out. And when deciphering rules and regulations of ports and docks, or regulations of shipping manuals, her keen eye could swiftly read through a page of complex regulations; and after a very short space of time she would then get some paper and write down the most important parts of the article she had read and would retain the rest in her head.

She would say 'you only remember what's important to you', yet she retained a vast knowledge of shipping regulations in her head which she could quote at the appropriate time.

This chapter gives the details of a ordinary sailing life for Kate Tyrrell on board the *Denbighshire Lass*.

The *Denbighshire Lass* required some expensive repairs to be carried out while at Connah's Quay that year, 1888, and Kate made a journey to meet the people who were going to be doing the necessary work; she knew exactly what was to be done as she had inspected the hull herself, and knew to the penny what the work would cost. She also wanted to look into what might be involved in changing the *Denbighshire Lass*'s rigging from schooner to ketch rigged.

She brought her paperwork and official documents down into the skipper's cabin on the stern of the ship. Kate left no stone unturned. She inspected everything, even the crew's cabin in the ship's bow.

Before she could set sail, Kate needed to plot her course. The navigational charts of the day were called blue-backed charts. This chart, which was carried by all vessels, was enormous in size. It was similar to a large roll of wallpaper, but two to three feet in width, and usually only the relevant section was unfolded. Like a geological map of Europe, it also had relevant information about the Channel et cetera, and details of all the various lighthouses. This information was extremely scanty by today's standards of Decca navigation, and frequently ships sailed into unknown waters. Kate, with the help of a ruler and compass, examined this blue-backed chart before and during all voyages. The relevant section would be spread over the skipper's table and then examined in great detail. Kate prided herself on her skill in plotting a course, and she would also log, from the chart and speed logs, the location of the ship at any time during the journey. Because Kate was so insistent on everything being shipshape, she had a special shelf made to hold this gigantic roll of a chart, which was normally kept on the deck of the skipper's cabin.

After course plotting with the blue-backed chart, and checking that the magnetic compass and sails were in working order, the next task was to determine what the weather would be like for the trip. It is very difficult for us to imagine today, but the tradesmen who built these ships and the sailors who sailed them could tell what the weather would be like by examining cloud movements and the stars. Given their primitive tools, they were extremely accurate. Granted, mistakes could be made, but more often than not, sailors were accurate. Their lives, after all, depended on their skill: wind conditions were crucial to the survival of a sailing craft.

When heading for Cardiff or down channel, all vessels had to head for the Smalls lighthouse and make their way from there. The Smalls lighthouse was identified, like all other lighthouses, by the amount of flashes given by its lamp. All lighthouses and treacherous stretches of coastline were marked on the blue-backed chart.

After following all these procedures and plotting a course, Kate then got the ship's speed logs. She examined the dials before placing them on the draw lines, and then cast them over the stern of the ship when sail was set.

Then they were underway.

The ship's wheel was on the deck, out in all weathers, so that the sails could be observed all the time by the person steering the ship. If the sails were not full, the course could be changed by tacking, that is, taking a zig-zag line of sailing to ensure maximum wind power.

The captain's log book was kept in the sailor's lock-up while the ship was in port, and would be laid on the table throughout the voyage, as all the ship's journeys had to be recorded. On this trip, some of the voyage would be documented by Kate herself. She prided herself on this fact.

After some hours at sea, Kate would examine the blue-backed chart, then go to the stern of the vessel, haul in the ship's speed logs, and examine the dials to determine the ship's nautical mileage. She would then return to the cabin, examine the chart again, and with great accuracy, pinpoint on the chart exactly where they were. The information was then logged in the skipper's log book. She would repeat this exercise frequently. On the completion of the journey, on port entry, officials of Lloyds would come on board and examine the captain's log book for the contents. All had to be correct.

As they entered Connah's Quay, Kate had just been on duty on the wheel. Each crew member took his turn, and Kate demanded no special treatment. Kate always quoted the story of the sailor who could not read or write, but who was very clever and had will and ability. His company saw his potential and had him taught, upon which he became a master mariner, sought after by all the big shipping companies. As the crew's employer, Kate was strict, a real stickler for detail, and kept a good eye on the men.

After docking at Connah's Quay, Kate saw that the journey had taken twelve hours. It was late, so the crew rested. At daybreak the next morning, Kate made her way to the shipbuilder's yard to further her enquiries about ship repairs and rigging changes. She could see quite a number of Norwegian and Russian ships in the harbour, something that was quite common in that day and age. Many of these ships carried the wives of the crew. As she made her way from the ship across the various makeshift ramps to the quayside she carrying her small case folder marked *Denbighshire Lass*. This folder held all the documents Kate was to need for the trip. Making her way along the cobblestone wharf, she finally arrived at the ship repair yard and, with her usual swiftness, she was discussing her business of the ship's repair with the shipwrights. This exercise would have taken three to four hours. Kate seemed to be able to retain vast amounts of information in her head about the business side of things. When in consultation with the shipwrights about hull repairs, she would quote lengths of planks, dimensions, and costs. The ship's carpenter foremen dealing with this would have to substantiate her quotes by looking at the plans, but Kate did not need to look at them. She carried everything in her head and drove a very hard bargain – Kate would then quote costs of repairs from the last voyage, and compare the costs of this present job.

And so it was back to the vessel, which by now had been unloaded of timber props cargo. The *Denbighshire Lass* was now being loaded with bricks from the quarry. If

41

Kate spotted a schooner similar to the *Denbighshire Lass* but with extra sails and or anything else she thought would be an advantage to the *Denbighshire*, she would not hesitate to ask the owners of the craft all about it.

The repairs were duly carried out and inspected by Kate, as indeed were the costs – she was acutely aware of the business side of the shipping industry, as always. This particular voyage lasted three weeks, after which the Denbighshire Lass was homeward bound.

Whenever Kate was on board, everything was always shipshape. She always prided herself on what she called good sea legs and no problems of sea sickness. She was always immaculate about the ship signals NBQM, and these letters were on all correspondence: any reference to the ship would always read 'Denb. Lass NBQM 61 ton, owner Kate Tyrrell', later to be registered in Lloyds as No. 20559. Now she plotted the course expertly, taking readings like the experienced sailor she was. The sea was calm, but there was a heavy fog, which made the ship appear ghostly and eerie, although that never fazed Kate. All that could be seen were the lights of distant schooners, and the air was filled only with the faraway sound of foghorns and the creaking of the masts and rigging of her own ship. But as sunrise approached, the fog lifted to reveal the Irish coast. The *Denbighshire Lass* was headed for Arklow port. The harbour, shrouded in fog, would be disaster for any ship with a bigger tonnage – such vessels had to seek shelter in Wicklow harbour before the weather would allow them to enter Arklow. However, the little schooner found no difficulty there.

Laurence Brennan – and Kate – made many voyages over the years to Connah's Quay and Liverpool. They had no problems finding crews – times were still very hard and men were desperate for work. Some men, though, maintained that small vessels such as the *Denbighshire Lass* were death traps, and were reluctant to go coasting, preferring to take their chances in the clippers that sailed foreign waters. But times were such that some men were always to be found. During this time the trading of the *Denbighshire Lass* was as good as could be expected. Like all industries, however, it was governed by the unstable political climate at the time. She needed to look for ways to expand her business.

In 1884 and 1885 steam ships had already started to replace small vessels, and all competed to carry the same cargo. Now times were not easy. The *Denbighshire Lass* sailed Irish routes – to Dungarvan, to Waterford, and also to her home registered port of Dublin. She also did much more unusual trading. For instance, on several trips the *Denbighshire Lass* had brought bricks and tiles, delivered from Buckley Bricks and Tiles to the river by horse-drawn cart – horse power was used for off-loading and on-loading most cargoes – and loaded there. There was a great demand for bricks and tiles from Spain and Portugal, particularly Bilbao, as well as from Ireland, and on the return voyage from the Iberian Peninsula, the *Denbighshire Lass* would carry a cargo of iron ore. Many schooners similar to the *Denbighshire Lass* did the continental run from Connah's Quay to Ireland with floor tiles and bricks, and it was not uncommon for coasters this size to be caught off guard by the weather and to be lost with all cargo. It was a difficult and dangerous business.

The flourishing brick and tile trade saw small coasters, schooners, ketches, along with some steam ships, all sailing to areas along the east coast of Ireland; not just Dublin and upward towards Belfast, but also to Wexford, Cork, Waterford, and Dungarvan. Land drainage, piping, and all types of sanitary hardware were common general coasting cargoes then, along with coal, which would be brought by some of the larger vessels, though smaller ships would also carry coal when necessary. These items of cargo were easily damaged, and the slow-sailing coasters were therefore the preferred method of transport of the brick and tile companies.

Therefore, despite the threat of steam, at Connah's Quay there was always a forest of masts. Schooners, ketches (vessels with tall mainmast and smaller mizzen, both rigged with gaff and boom sails; the ketches being easier to look after than schooners), brigs, brigantines, barques, and barquentines were all to be seen. The sight of all these ships fully rigged and heading out to sea one after the other must have been a sight to behold.

Two years earlier, in 1886 – about the time of Edward Tyrrell's funeral – many experts had gathered in Arklow to discuss the possibility of building a munitions factory there and to examine a possible site on North Quay – near the original premises of the Arklow manure works. The proposed Kynoch's factory would create a great deal of employment and, Kate knew, an increased demand for shipping. She kept an interested eye on the proceedings.

All things considered, Kate was now worried about the unrestful climate in Ireland with murmurs of trouble and more trouble to follow.

The voyaging and crew lists of the vessel for this period, signed on 3 January 1889, read as follows:

Crew	Year of Birth	Capacity	Town
Laurence Brennan	1838	Master	Arklow
Edward Kavanagh	1834	Mate	Arklow
Robert Kavanagh	1869	AB	Arklow
Samuel Brennan	1872	Boy	Arklow

Account of Voyages

Sailed from Liverpool 6th July 1888
Arrive Arklow 10th July
Sailed from Arklow 17th July
Arrive Cardiff 19th July
Sailed from Cardiff 25th July
Arrive New Ross 6th August
Sailed from New Ross 15th August
Arrive Bristol 18th August
Sailed from Bristol 31st August
Arrive Swansea 2nd September
Sailed from Swansea 12th September
Arrive Fiddown 15th September
Sailed from Fiddown 1st October
Arrive Swansea 6th October
Sailed from Swansea 14th October
Arrive New Ross 17th October
Sailed from New Ross 1st November
Arrive Bristol 5th November
Sailed from Bristol 14th November
Arrive Newport 14th November
Sailed from Newport 19th November
Arrive Wexford 10th December 1888.

Received at Wexford Port 3rd January 1889.

This crew list shows that Laurence's son Sam was again on board. While John Fitzpatrick sailed on the *Denbighshire Lass* for this voyage, he also sailed other ships on other routes and sometimes was skipper of other vessels which he would join at Wexford and New Ross ports.

The list outlined above also shows that the *Denbighshire Lass* sailed during the winter months. This in itself was not unusual, weather permitting, but on numerous occasions vessels like the *Denbighshire Lass* would have to remain port bound. Sailing was just too dangerous in wild weather.

The amount of voyaging put a great deal of demand on the crew in terms of hard work and manpower but, as previously noted, these demands were the accepted normal duties of such a craft in these times.

A ship's crew could join the *Denbighshire Lass* from any of the ports where she traded, not just from Arklow. Many crews were acquired in ports like Garston, Swansea, Glasgow, before the *Denbighshire Lass* would sail to a new port, where some of the crew would then be discharged and new crew members taken on board. This was all quite normal practice, as labour was in abundance.

The account of voyages shows that the *Denbighshire Lass* was contracted to bring coal from Cardiff in July 1888. Usually such a cargo was brought to Wexford, Waterford or Courtown rather than Arklow. The voyage from Arklow to Cardiff normally took two days, and with bad weather two and a half days. The course to Cardiff could prove tricky in bad weather from the Irish Sea into the Bristol Channel, past Lundy, past the Smalls, and onward to the river Severn entrance. As usual, a crew of three – skipper, mate and cook – was on board the *Denbighshire Lass* for this voyage. All three crew members were also able to repair the sails when needed.

The *Denbighshire Lass*, although sixty-one tons registered, could carry 120 tons of cargo. Upon entering Cardiff, the port of the ship was moved into an area where coal would be brought by horse-drawn cart to load her. Sometimes this loading was carried out by a plank or running system: horses carrying coal in baskets would be brought down one full side of the ship; then their load would be discharged and the horse would walk up the other side unladen.

This was a very slow process and sometimes, to speed things up, a special loading wharf was provided in some areas. The ship moored underneath this wharf and a full cartload of coal was off-loaded from above. This loading of cargo took three days. After the cargo was on board and battened down, the *Denbighshire Lass* took to sea again.

Even fast vessels like the *Denbighshire Lass* were slow at moving cargoes with a high slag content as damp slag could damage the ship in bad weather, proving disastrous for little schooners. Leaving Cardiff port, bad weather also made entering the Bristol Channel difficult and dangerous. Many schooners met a watery grave right near the Smalls, in the Bristol Channel. This was by far a more awkward course than sailing to North Cumbria and to the Cumberland Basin, and more difficult than the straightforward Garston docks, but there was a good crew on the *Denbighshire Lass* and this journey proved no problem to them.

Once the *Denbighshire Lass* arrived at her destination with the coal, the off-loading process was extremely slow. Baskets of coal were hoisted to the deck and dockhands did their best, wheeling the coal in barrows down planks to a coal yard near where the ship entered Arklow port. As well as being slow, off-loading was a dangerous – and expensive – process: if any of the workers slipped from the plank and lost the wheelbarrow, both the barrow and its contents would have to be paid for. This proved a problem.

In some cases shipping merchants had an agreement whereby the workers off-loading the likes of the *Denbighshire Lass* would get paid in groceries and other goods, rather than in cash. Kate paid her crew a wage of £2 a month – considering that a pint of beer cost fourpence, a shilling could go a long way. A worker who lost a barrow and coal because of high winds and other factors beyond his control would get fewer goods in return for his work, with the outcome that his whole family suffered.

A vessel like the *Denbighshire Lass* would have to

carry ballast at all times during her voyages. Otherwise, were the ship to sail unladen, her construction meant that she would capsize very quickly. Hence, when arriving in a port, a new cargo was taken on board for the outbound journey as soon as possible after the old cargo had been discharged. This rule applied to all vessels like the *Denbighshire Lass*, of registered 61 tons up to 200 tons, as they were all constructed from a similar design.

Port regulations varied from place to place. Some ports along Connah's Quay had rules which gave steamers first preference over schooners such as the *Denbighshire Lass*. In these early years before plimsoll line regulations, some ships, particularly wooden craft, could be very easily overloaded, which meant that the ship would very easily go aground in shallow water. Frequently this would also result in the vessel becoming waterlogged until she would finally keel over and be irretrievable. Sometimes the same problem would occur in fog, and often these catastrophes would happen because of cargo shifting, making it impossible to control the boat in bad weather.

While the *Denbighshire Lass* pursued the coasting trade under skipper Laurence Brennan, Kate, though really the owner, was required by her father's instructions to share the business with her remaining sister Ellen. Both sisters were contemplating marriage at about this time, and now Ellen made her decision. She married and became Mrs Hyland; and when she moved away from her original home, as promised, Kate received her share of the coasting business. Kate Tyrrell was now the sole owner of the *Denbighshire Lass*.

John James Fitzpatrick, then aged twenty-six, had sailed the vessel as mate to Laurence Brennan, and was listed on the crew list on some occasions as Jimmy Fitzpatrick. John and Kate were to become very good friends and confidantes. All this work and time spent away from home had meant that Kate, unlike most young women of her time, was unable to consider marriage. She had too much to do to keep her schooner business busy and viable, and she threw herself relentlessly into this work. As they sailed together with Laurence Brennan (now fifty-one and still listed on many of the shipping documents as master and owner of the ship) during the years 1889-1891, they would gather together in the stern cabin and discuss the coasting trade together. All of them were concerned with enhancing trade and deciding on the best, most viable and profitable routes. Each of them was knowledgeable in this area, and the business was becoming a success.

The *Denbighshire Lass* voyages during 1889 and early 1890 are as follows:

Account of Crew

Name	Year of Birth	Capacity Engaged	Town
Laurence Brennan	1838	Master	Arklow
Edward Kavanagh	1834	Mate	Arklow
Robert Kavanagh	1869	AB	Arklow
Samuel Brennan	1872	Boy	Arklow

Account of Voyages
Sailed from Liverpool 6th July 1888
Arrive Arklow 10th July
Sailed from Arklow 17th July
Arrive Cardiff 19th July
Sailed from Cardiff 25th July
Arrive New Ross 6th August
Sailed from New Ross 15th August
Arrive Bristol 18th August

Sailed from Bristol 31st August
Arrive Swansea 2nd September
Sailed from Swansea 12th September
Arrive Fiddown 15th September
Sailed from Fiddown 1st October
Arrive Swansea 6th October
Sailed from Swansea 14th October
Arrive New Ross 17th October
Sailed from New Ross 1st November
Arrive Bristol 5th November
Sailed from Bristol 14th November
Arrive Newport 14th November
Sailed from Newport 19th November
Arrive Wexford 10th December 1888.

Received at Wexford Port 3rd January 1889.

Signed: Master Laurence Brennan.

The Board of Trade official document regarding both crew and ship on List D, as described above, was to change format in 1890 and would from then on be headed: 'Official Log Book and Accounts of Voyages and Crew'. This new format of ship accounts would be far more comprehensive and cover such detail as draught water reading and free board midships. There was also a new section covering births and deaths on board.

While the *Denbighshire Lass* was registered in Dublin, the rules specified that registration of a ship could be carried out in any port which had a custom house, for example Dublin, Cork or Waterford. But all merchant vessels were under the auspices of the Crown, hence the flying of the Red Ensign (Union Jack) by all merchant shipping which were registered in Britain or West Britain (a name by which Ireland was known). As shipping levy was also duly paid to the Crown, it was unheard of in those days for any ship to fly the Irish Tricolour nautical flag.

It was around this time, 1890, that the south pier in Arklow was first constructed. Ships of 200 ton, far larger than any ship which could previously use the port, could now moor in the Avoca river.

Kate Tyrrell was still pursuing the possibilities of having her name listed on shipping official documents as managing owner of the vessel, and was finding it very difficult. But 1890 was to start a gradual change in attitudes to and the rights of women. For the first time women began to agitate for the right to suffrage – a word which gave rise to the term Suffragist, which later became Suffragettes. As the unequal rights given to women at the time did not permit them to own any real property (it was automatically the property of their husbands) Laurence Brennan's name still remained on some of the *Denbighshire Lass*'s shipping documents as managing owner.

In the year 1890, Kate's friend John Fitzpatrick again sailed as mate on the vessel with his uncle Laurence Brennan, skipper. There was a lot of trading during this time between Liverpool and Glasgow, a route Kate's vessel often sailed. There were some repairs to the ship to be carried out at Connah's Quay. After these repairs were carried out, the vessel traded between Troon (Scotland), Carrickfergus, and Belfast during 1891.

The year 1891 saw the *Denbighshire Lass* sail to Swansea and as far as Glasgow. She had no fixed route. Like all schooners scrabbling for business in stiff competition, she went wherever there was a cargo to be loaded.

According to the Archive Records: Official Log Book and Accounts of Voyages and Crew, the *Denbighshire Lass* voyages during 1892 were as follows:

Account of Crew

Name	Year of Birth	Capacity Engaged	Town
Laurence Brennan	1839	Master	Arklow
John Dempsey	1832	Mate	Arklow
William Ford	1871	Mate	Arklow
Laurence Byrne	1870	AB	Arklow
John Fitzgerald	1874	Cook	Arklow

Account of Voyages

Trading between Cardiff, Dublin, New Ross, and Glasgow.

1st January 1892 Cardiff
30th June 1892 Glasgow.

Received at Glasgow port 30th July 1892.

Signed: Laurence Brennan.

The year 1893, which saw the British Women's Rights' Movement in motion for the first time, was the beginning of some changes in attitudes towards women; and Kate would finally succeed in getting her name on some shipping documents as ship owner.

At the same time, her friendship with the mate of the *Denbighshire Lass* had now become strong, and they began to think of marriage.

The voyage accounts of the vessel for 1893 read as follows:

Name	Year of Birth	Capacity Engaged	Town
Laurence Brennan	1839	Master	Arklow
Jimmy Fitzpatrick	1863	Mate	Arklow
PatrickProctor	1873	AB	Arklow
John Chatem	1876	Boy	Arklow
James Brennan	1878	Boy	Arklow

Account of Voyages
September 24th 1893, Wicklow to Liverpool
October 15th 1893, Liverpool to Dublin
October 29th 1893, Dublin to Killough
November 19th 1893, Killough to Glasgow
December 11th 1893, Glasgow to Newry.

The above voyage crew list incorporates Laurence's son James Brennan, fifteen years old (Laurence himself was now fifty-four), along with John Fitzpatrick as mate.

The following year, 1894, after some more voyages as mate, John was to become master of the *Denbighshire Lass*, though Kate as owner obviously had the last word when it came to the ship. From then on it was this formidable team of Kate and John who would look after the *Denbighshire Lass*. John Fitzpatrick, or John Patrick as he was named by those who knew him, was to become a close business confidant of Kate's, and any decisions regarding the vessel were decided on a mutual basis. Their own relationship was also growing more intimate.

That year more repairs were needed at Connah's Quay. While on board, homeward bound back to Ireland, Kate would leave the cabin after examining the blue-backed chart, and then go on deck. If she was to observe some tie rope not correct on the sails, she would immediately go and tie it herself. She knew all the knots for ropes and, though she had feminine hands, a knot or reef she tied was as tight as any seaman would make it.

Always while on deck, she would look around at the sky and attempt to predict the weather on the basis of its colour, the clouds and so on. 'There's bad weather coming from the north east and we may just miss it if the wind keeps up,' she would say, or 'Batten down the hatches, we're going to be caught by unsettling winds.' Like all other experienced mariners at that time, she had an astounding degree of accuracy in her judgements.

She used the ship's brass telescope when looking for weather signs. She would examine any ship on the horizon with the telescope and make out firstly what type of craft the ship was, and then what flag she flew. All British and Irish ships at this time flew what was referred to as the Red Ensign (Union Jack). Kate resented this, but it would be many years before the Irish Tricolour could be flown.

She always had the sails rigged for maximum sea speed while tacking. On deck, she had flat shoes and a type of gaberdine garb (woollen hat) which she always said came from Australia.

John Fitzpatrick wore a peaked captain's cap on board, though on this particular trip, John was not well and stayed in his cabin for the rest of the trip. He would listen to reports of Kate's sightings from the deck. Down below he kept a shoemaker's last – like many other men at the time, he would repair all their shoes, including Kate's. She would always wear low heels on board – as she said, 'You cannot walk around on deck with so much high heel.' But she was very surefooted. Dressed in her heavy coat and the gaberdine hat over her unruly black curls, she must have been an unusual sight.

When Kate entered the captain's cabin, under the ship's wheel at the stern, she always replaced the telescope in the sailor's lock-up (sailor's chest). This was a large wooden container made of oak, with ropes on each side. The telescope, as she said, was a precision instrument and, like the sextant, was wrapped up in a very fine cloth and placed carefully on a shelf in the sailor's chest.

From the deck could be heard the stretching of the sailing ropes and the sound of the starboard and port diaptrex lights swinging. Kate would then sit down at the skipper's table and examine her business papers which she took from her folder marked '*Denbighshire Lass* NBQM'. This work would be carried out by the light of a kerosene (paraffin) lamp, of which there were two in the cabin. These lamps gave off a greeny-white glow and also some heat. The smell of paraffin must have evaporated through the deck, if not through the timber bulkhead, as there never seemed to be a choking paraffin smell in the cabin.

Kate was pleased with all the ship's repairs that had been carried out. They were absolutely necessary if the ship was to be seaworthy. It took a lot of her thriftiness to be able to afford these repairs and keep the ship coasting. But Kate was careful when it came to money. As she always used to say 'Take care of the pennies and the pounds will take care of themselves'. But this was 1894. Times were extremely hard and she always kept the hard word to all connected with the *Denbighshire Lass*.

That morning Kate had been at the wheel and carried out the course plotting after a night of heavy fog and mist. Now she went on deck again to find a very cold bright day, with ample wind filling the sails. As the ship began to head for the Irish coastline, the sea was quite calm. The *Denbighshire Lass* began veering southwards to Dungarvan, where she was to offload some of the bricks and tiles she carried. As she headed down the coast, Kate remembered the metal men at Tramore which she had often seen on sailing trips to Cork.

The smell of fresh tar on the deck, and sea air, combined with the smell of cooking from the cabin below, would make anyone feel they were starving. Some of the crew used to bring pairs of rabbits on board with them and make them into a most appetising stew. However, this particular morning, the smell of cooking was that of some fish and meat that Kate had been given aboard a Norwegian ketch which had been moored alongside the *Denbighshire Lass* while at Connah's Quay. Though all hands got a share of whatever was being cooked, someone had to be at the wheel at all times. Kate always made sure that she ate last, so that no one could say she gave herself an easy time. She usually said, 'Let the crew have their meal first.' She believed strongly in basic needs. She always said 'Keep warm, don't overindulge in anything and get some food.'

On mooring at Dungarvan, Kate would go ashore to take care of shipping business, always carrying her *Denbighshire Lass* folder. Again, she knew exactly where to go to see the port authority people. All the *Denbighshire Lass* paperwork and the ship's log book were up to date, and all various ship's log entries and particulars had been scrutinised by Kate while on board, as she knew how strict the port authority people were. Also, some of the English customs officials in these ports and docks were over strict, and were inclined to treat the Irish ship and schooner with a suspect eye. Kate was very cool dealing with the port custodians; she never let her feelings show and always had her ship, as she said, 'shipshape'. She spoke to them with her usual businesslike approach. Her papers were in order always. Although she was not always happy with the situation, she did not see a change ever coming about, since many Irish men were working either across the water in Britain or were in the British navy or army.

On this occasion John was with Kate as she walked to the Dungarvan port offices. After transacting all her business at the port office, she told John she would meet him back on board. They always made a point to be back on board ship before dark, as sometimes the port authorities were strict about this. John left her and went to collect food supplies for the homeward journey.

On the way back to the quayside where the *Denbighshire Lass* was moored, Kate could see that the vast majority of the ships there – at least eighty per cent – were flying the Red Ensign (the Union Jack). All Kate's shipping documents were stamped with the official British Merchant Navy's stamp. To be forced to deal with these people in her own country offended Kate, though she could not see what she would do about it. The British port authority's presence in both the regular and merchant Navy seemed to be one of these 'no solution' problems.

During 1894, there was a lot of talk about unrest among the Irish people. While Ireland was frequently referred to as 'West Britain', the locals had a tense feeling when dealing with people in authority. Very many people at the time spoke Irish – though not so many as had spoken it before the Famine – and they were being told to learn English if they were to acquire work under this existing system. Irish people seemed to be losing interest in their native language during this time. Certainly, since the school system was administered by the British, the language was not taught in schools. It must have been a most peculiar situation in that parents, who spoke only Irish, to have their children speaking what was to them a foreign language.

But for Kate, business was business, and she had a ship to run. On making her way back to the *Denbighshire Lass*, she could see the schooners and vessels being discharged and loaded. Some of them were being off-loaded with wooden kegs of Guinness, and a large number of them were off-loading coal, while small ketches and schooners like the *Denbighshire Lass* were taking on board small cargoes of coal.

The smell of tar was extremely strong as many of the vessels were having their hulls coated with bitumen to protect them against the adverse weather and seafaring journeys. The quay was full of men smoking pipes, and port authority personnel keeping an eye out for anything out of place.

Kate, with her usual swiftness, was back on board the ship to inspect all the sails that had to be repaired. As they were to stay another day in Dungarvan, Kate knew that there would be ample time to repair the sails which had become damaged with bad weather. All equipment for repairing the sails was kept by the crew in their cabin in a smaller, but similar, lock-up sailor's chest (similar to the one in the skipper'scabin).

When John Fitzpatrick arrived on board, dusk had already fallen and so immediately the kerosene lamps and the starboard and port lamps illuminated. The ship's crew had been taking care of the cargo, off-loading and on-loading, during the absence of skippers John and Kate.

The next day, after the off-loading and on-loading of cargoes had finally been completed, and when the sails had been repaired, the *Denbighshire Lass* would set sail for Arklow. It had been a busy trip and a tiring one. John Fitzpatrick skippered the ship while Kate stayed in the cabin examining business papers.

She could feel the turbulence of the ship as they left the river estuary and entered the the sea. She then left the cabin and went on deck to see Dungarvan port fading towards the stern of the ship.

As the century drew to a close, competition for work was very stiff among the various shipping companies. As well as the usual cargoes of coal, bricks and tiles, textiles and more, which were brought to ports such as Courtown and Dungarvan, ships were also increasingly involved in transporting timber from the shores of Ireland to the coal mines in Wales, to feed the incessant demand for coal created by the burgeoning factories that relied on steam power.

While this was a most worthwhile business, many seaworthy schooner merchants had their eye on trade between Dublin and Belfast, as these areas were flourishing more than any others on the island.

Belfast's huge Harland & Wolfe shipyard, in operation since the early 1800s, employed more than 10,000 men. The city also dominated the linen industry, and was the core of Irish manufacturing. It was also noticeable for an increasing split between the Catholic and Protestant communities. While Dublin had a sizeable population of some 400,000 people, it was not as industrialised as Belfast, but was seen more as an administrative centre.

The *Denbighshire Lass* brought coal from Cardiff, Swansea and Newport to the factories of Belfast, returning to Dublin with textiles, bricks and tiles. This was a profitable run, but necessitated cross-channel and coasting voyages from Belfast down the east coast of Ireland.

At the time the schooners like the *Denbighshire Lass* could be sailed by three or four people, usually skipper, mate, and two boys. Wages for the crew were £3 a month. The mate would normally have half a crown more, and sometimes as much as seven or eight shillings more.

At the same time the coastal trade was flourishing, railways were being built all over Ireland, bringing with them all kinds of new foodstuffs and an influx of people. The famous Dublin tram, however, would not appear for many years to come.

In 1895 and 1896, Kate made few voyages, and those she did were usually home runs to Dungarvan: she was increasingly in demand to look after the administration of the business in Arklow, and she had great confidence in John Fitzpatrick's ability to master the vessel.

John and Kate, although they had a strong business and personal relationship, were very different. Kate had a fiery personality; John on the other hand was a very quiet and easygoing man, and it appears that he was happy to let Kate dictate how things should be run on board ship. But opposites often attract, and Kate and John were good shipping partners, a relationship they cemented in 1896 when, finally, they married.

That year, Kate was very keen to convert the *Denbighshire Lass* to ketch rigging, something she had been considering for many years. Ketch-rigged ships were faster and easier to manage than schooners, and they became very common, especially as fishing boats. She decided that she would acquire the mizzen and tall main mast for the *Denbighshire Lass* by the turn of the century.

The years 1896 and 1897 were to see the *Denbighshire* complete more of the tramp trading on both the Irish and British coastline from the River Clyde to the Bristol Channel, to the banks of the Lee at Cork, and the river Dee at Connah's Quay. By 1895 the *Denbighshire Lass* had been thirty-eight years at sea and once again required some extensive repairs, for which she sailed again to Connah's Quay with John Fitzpatrick as master. It was a priority of Kate's to have the ship in perfect condition in order to be able to compete effectively with the small steamers now struggling for their share of the shipping trade. The repairs were completed at Connah's Quay, and the transaction again by Kate. The *Denbighshire Lass* now sailed to Liverpool where she moored in Langton Dock and Runcorn, where not only the masts of brigs and barques could be seen but, increasingly, steel ships. There was also a great deal of trading now between Connah's Quay in Liverpool (England) and Glasgow in Scotland. With Troon, these were the main destinations of the *Denbighshire Lass*.

The trade grew ever more relentless so that, by 1899, the *Denbighshire Lass* was now sailing during the winter months she had been used to spending idle. But for Kate, things had never been better – her ship was now registered (under her maiden name, naturally) on most shipping documents, and when on board, she sailed with her partner and her husband, John Fitzpatrick. She had become a force to be reckoned with.

Chapter 8

COURTOWN AND THE LIGHTERS

While on cargo runs from Britain to Dungarvan, the *Denbighshire Lass* would frequently have to call to Courtown on her return trip to discharge small cargoes.
It was during these visits of small cargo off-loading that a reliable open-ended contract was drawn up to bring coal from Connah's Quay, Bridgewater, and other areas of Britain directly to Courtown for the coal yards there. During this period in Courtown, Redmond's and Connor's were the only coal yards in the area. The particular time of the year for these voyages usually ran from the months of March to September and then recommenced the following year.

While the *Denbighshire Lass* was of small tonnage, she was much too large to enter Courtown Harbour and, therefore, the cargo was discharged to a smaller craft which in turn brought it to shore. When the *Denbighshire Lass* would arrive at Courtown with coal to be discharged, this small craft called the lighter would moor alongside her. The lighter was manned by four or five men and was twenty-five to twenty-eight feet in length, and was rowed from the shore to a larger vessel. The men manning the lighter would also be the muscle behind the off-loading of the cargo.

The lighter could take up to one ton (twenty sacks of coal), but was very seldom laden to this capacity.

The sacks of coal were manhandled from the *Denbighshire Lass's* hold and on to the lighter. After some time, when the crew of the lighter had loaded up, they would then row to shore where a man operated a winch at the shore side from a tripod. The coal was then winched up from the lighter and placed in a horse and car, sack by sack. The horse and car would then make its way to either Connor's quay or Redmond's coal yard to be unloaded for distribution later.

The horse and car would then return to the quayside and the lighter and crew would once more row out to the *Denbighshire Lass*. The whole process began all over again until the *Denbighshire* was fully discharged.

The crew of the lighter were paid two pennies per ton for this back-breaking work. This wage also applied to the man who owned the horse and car. The local council controlled the lighter craft, but the man who owned the horse and car was his own boss. Owing to the amount of sacks, and wear and tear involved in this regular coal discharging exercise, many women were employed to make and repair the coal sacks. This was a full-time job, and a lot of sack making was carried out during the winter months to prepare for the coming March when the coal would start to arrive by schooners like the *Denbighshire Lass*.

Kate would always watch this process. Like the formidable lady she always was, she emphasised to the crew's skipper John that the ship must be cleaned off very well after the coal unloading operation. And as previously mentioned, her instructions were always carried out to the letter. After giving such a command, Kate would always check the weather by looking skyward to north, south, east and west. 'There's strong winds due,' she would deduce, or 'Another great day for sailing tomorrow.'

There were quite a number of vessels trading to Courtown at the time, ships like the *Dorothy Watson, Witch, Emmie Alice, Lapwing, Mylady* and the *Isabel*, et cetera, and later ships like the *Angus Craig* and the *Deangate*. Many of these crafts were skippered for years by Arklow men on their voyages to Courtown.

During these early years, one of the landmarks visible was the tripod for removing sacks of coal from the lighters, and there were many paintings and drawings of Courtown depicting this scene. When the time of year came around when there would be no more off-loading of coal until the following year, the men who manned the lighters would then work at their usual occupations which were usually trawling and fishing.

Kate was on several of these voyages from Britain to Courtown and had made trips ashore here quite often. As in Connah's Quay, one could see at Courtown a forest of masts of brigs, barks, schooners, ketches, and quite a lot of steamers also. It was not unusual for the *Denbighshire Lass* to carry other commodities to Courtown, such as tiles and bricks. All of these small sailing craft were the only reliable way of transferring breakable/fragile cargoes, such as pottery, because of their slow speed.

Harbour regulations and bye laws varied from port to port and Kate looked after all of this. The cost of breaking harbour regulations could range from ten shillings up to five pounds.

Sometimes the route from Connah's Quay to Courtown could be a tough trip, but the *Denbighshire Lass* was now a tough old lady. Steam, iron, and steel ships were on the way to replace these wooden craft, but schooners like the

Denbighshire Lass were not willingly going to give up a whole way of life and tradition. It has been said that schooners like her would often have to show how good they were by battling against waves higher than their main masts upon crossing the channel. It was a time, as they said, of 'iron men in wooden boats'.

It could be extremely rough on a schooner like the *Denbighshire Lass* when tacking, as most of the journey could be spent, both night and day, hauling on ropes for sail changes. During this exercise, sleep must have been minimal with waves bashing on the hull near where any of the crew were resting, plus the never ending creaking and cracking sound of the timber in the ship's structure. Yet there were few stories of sea sickness. Hauling and pulling sail ropes was a full time job on a ship such as the *Denbighshire Lass*.

The off-loading of cargo at Courtown could mean that the ship would lay at anchor overnight and, after the lighters discharging all night, the ship could then slip anchor and head homeward bound, hoping for a fair breeze to fill the sails.

As a young man, I went with my mother Lily to Courtown to look at trading records of the *Denbighshire Lass*, which were in a house owned by a Mr Redmond. I was fascinated by all of this, particularly with the accuracy and legibility of the logbook entries which were all penned in the most impressive copperplate handwriting. Mr Redmond seemed to have all the records of maritime Courtown, and he also knew my mother Lily and my grandfather John Fitzpatrick. We seemed to talk for hours and hours about ships of yesteryear. He had all kinds of items relating to Courtown Harbour and ships. For example, he had bye laws, regulations, and penalties of Courtown Harbour dating back to 1903. He had lists of costs for transporting goods of import such as bacon, coal (six old pence per ton, I remember), groceries, butter, and also the cost of the pilot's work on the ships. I remember him saying that the Harbour Master of Courtown those days was a most hard-working man and his working hours were endless.

Mr Redmond seemed to have endless information; log books, documentation, and historical data of this period including paintings of Courtown Harbour done in the years 1860 to 1903. All of this I found most interesting and intriguing. He had such a profound knowledge on the area. I hope someone documents it, as it would be of great historical value for the future.

Some of the Arklow-connected ships to Courtown were as follows:

Ship	Master
Lapwing	J. Kearon
Denbighshire Lass	J. Fitzpatrick
Angus	Craig Kearons
Dorothy Watson	Thomas Fitzpatrick
Sea View	Hall

Some of John Fitzpatrick's relatives from Ballycanew also worked in Courtown during the days of the *Denbighshire Lass's* voyages, and they worked on both the trawlers and the lighters. Some of them would come on board the Denbighshire to visit John and Kate with news from the home place.

For John and Kate to visit Ballycanew at that time from Courtown would not have been impossible, as John did this. But with the inconvenience of going ashore, getting on a horse and trap from Courtown to Ballycanew, and then returning to the ship – bearing in mind that maybe on some occasions the *Denbighshire* would be off-loaded in a matter of hours – the journey would not be worth all the hassle.

Almost all of John Fitzpatrick's family had emigrated during the last few years of the century, but some relatives did remain in Ballycanew. Word of the whereabout of his brother Moses would filter back through the stories of merchant seamen, and it became known that he was now in Australia most of the time. A Chief Petty Officer in the British Navy, he had earlier come into contact with the Boxer Rebellion in China. This was an uprising that began in 1842 and was finally quashed by the forces of Britain, France, Russia, Japan, Germany, and the United States of America in 1900. One cause of the rebellion was that China did not like the idea of the British having such free-dom to trade from her ports. The Chinese always main-tained that foreign powers should be ousted. Much of the business life of China at the time was dominated by European powers, hence the presence of the Victoria Navy and Moses Fitzpatrick, Chief Petty Officer.

The close affiliation at that time between Britain and Australia through the Crown was such that the Australian Navy was known as the Victorian Navy, after the Australian state Victoria. The Australian Navy was only part of the worldwide contingent from the six world pow-ers which were amalgamated to quell this Boxer uprising. It must have been a navy of magnificent proportions for its day. This is where John Fitzpatrick's brother Moses had finally decided to be, in the Australian Navy, and he adopted Australia as his new home place.

Moses Fitzpatrick made it his business, as any good Wexford man would, to remain involved with his home place, and he joined a committee of Wexford people – they may have been from Hoboken, New York, and from other areas, but they were all Wexford men at heart, and they were responsible for the erection of a statue of Father

Murphy – a Wexfordman who had led the 1798 rebellion against the British – in what is now called the Parade Ground in Arklow. His name, along with those of the other committee members, is still listed on the plinth.

John and Kate had to take care of their usual business – the *Denbighshire Lass*, which was their livelihood. The vessel was now trading to Courtown with an open-ended contract for the usual commodities of cargo, along with some new runs to Belfast and Dublin ports. But business was such that each schooner of the day had to be very competitive. This being the case, Kate was now contemplating having her ship changed from a schooner-rigged to a ketch-rigged craft. All aspects of this had been given much thought before she finally decided to have these modifications carried out.

Chapter 9

A NEW CENTURY
– A NEW LIFE

The turn of the century was to bring another great change to Kate's life when, with the birth of her son James, she became a mother for the first time. With this new demanding child her life, she now stayed at home more often, but she determined that James would become familiar with shipping life and planned to bring him on board with her as often as possible – just as Edward Tyrrell had made her a part of his shipping life.

The official log book of voyages and crew for 1901 reads as follows:

Ship	Number	Port of Registration	Ton
Denbighshire Lass	20559	Dublin	61

Vessel lying up in Arklow for repairs from 1st January 1901 – 30th June 1901.

Signed: Master John Fitzpatrick.

The official log book entries of voyages and crew for late 1901 (ref. National Archives Records) is as follows:

Crew

Name	Year of Birth	Capacity Engaged	Town
John Fitzpatrick	1875	Master	Arklow
Peter Kearons	1878	Mate	Arklow
Peter Weadock	1880	AB	Arklow
Tim Byrne	1881	AB	Arklow
James Kenny	1873	Mate	Arklow
Michael English	1880	AB	Arklow
Patrick Tyrrell	1884	Cook	Arklow

Kearons, Weadock, Byrne discharged at Wicklow port. The rest of the crew remained.

Account of Voyages September to December 1901

From Arklow 12 September 1901
Arrive Liverpool 25 September 1901
From Liverpool 12 October 1901
Arrive Wicklow 15 October 1901
From Wicklow 23 October 1901
Arrive Garston 31 October 1901
From Garston 23 November 1901
Arrive Wexford 01 December 1901
From Wexford 13 December 1901
Arrive Barnstaple 25 December 1901

Received at port – Barnstaple.

Signed: John Fitzpatrick (Master), January 1902.

Competition was again extremely intense with vessels and small steamers, yet there seemed to be plenty for all as they carried out their voyaging. For example, 'The Official Log Book Entries and Accounts of Voyages and

Crew for 1904' reads as follows (ref. to Archives Records):

Name	Year of Birth	Capacity	Town	Ship
John Fitzpatrick	1865	Master	Arklow	D/Lass
William Greene	1860	Mate	Arklow	D/Lass
Michael Proctor	1868	A B	Arklow	D/Lass
John English	1872	Cook	Arklow	D/Lass
John Arthur	1862	Mate	Skerries	Foam
William Arthur	1860	Seaman	Skerries	Stag
Hugh McDermot	1882	Mate	Ramelton	Fortuna
Michael Gallagher	1879	Seaman	Ramelton	Mantura
Alex Hamill	1880	Cook	Cahoepoint	NoTenaght

Greene, Proctor, English, John and William Arthur discharged at Dublin. The rest of the crew remained on board.

Account of Voyages for 1904

From	To
Kilkeel 03/01/1904	Swansea 24/01/1904
Swansea 20/02/1904	Dublin 25/02/1904
Dublin 18/03/1904	Portrush 24/03/1904
Portrush 12/04/1904	Londonderry 12/04/1904
Londonderry 26/04/04	Belfast 27/04/1904
Belfast 03/05/1904	Romolton 06/05/1904

From	To
Romolton 23/05/1904	Connah's Quay 01/06/1904
Connah's Quay 08/06/1904	Haverford West 10/06/1904
Haverford West 20/06/1904	Newport Man 24/06/1904
Newport Man 28/06/1904	Cahoepoint 30/06/1904
Cahoepoint 05/07/1904	Newport Man 07/07/1904

Signed: John Fitzpatrick, 8th July 1904.

It can be seen that crew members were picked up at various ports and discharged for different runs outward bound to ports such as Belfast, Swansea, etc. Crew member William Greene appears to have been the husband of John Fitzpatrick's sister Julia. John's brother also sailed on the *Denbighshire Lass*, as did his son, who was cook. Coasting along must have been a real family affair, as was often the case in the merchant shipping business.

In 1905 Kate gave birth to a second child, a girl she named Elizabeth. However, the pregancy and birth were difficult, and both mother and child almost died; Kate was forty-two years old at the time and no longer as strong as she once had been. Subsequently Kate's health did improve somewhat, but she was never again the same active woman. She tended to remain ashore now whenever possible, looking after her family, continued to bring her children on board ship whenever possible. Her son was now five years old and a lively lad interested in running around the family's beloved schooner.

The *Denbighshire Lass* official account of Voyages and Crew for 1905 read as follows:

Name	Year of Birth	Capacity	Town	Ship
John Fitzpatrick	1866	Master	Arklow	D/Lass
James Kavanagh	1860	Mate	Arklow	D/Lass
Walter Lacey	1878	Seaman	Arklow	D/Lass
Thomas Kavanagh	1860	Cook	Arklow	D/Lass

Lacey and Kavanagh discharged at New Ross.

Account of Voyages

From	To
Newport 09/06/1904	Cahoepoint 15/06/1904
Cahoepoint 19/06/1904	Newport 09/07/1904
Newport 11/07/1904	Cahoepoint 13/07/1904
Cahoepoint 15/08/1904	Liverpool 20/08/1904
Liverpool 25/08/1904	Arklow 30/08/1904
Arklow 27/09/1904	Swansea 30/09/1904
Swansea 10/10/1904	Wexford 15/10/1904
Wexford 30/10/1904	Newport 05/11/1904
Newport 10/11/1904	New Ross 20/10/1904

Lying up at New Ross since 20th November 1904 coasting.

Signed: John Fitzpatrick, 10th January 1905.

The *Denbighshire Lass* had now been forty-eight years at sea, and was continually having repairs even of a small nature being carried out. The political climate in Ireland was such that lots of seafaring families, wherever possible, would have their spouses and children on board in order to be clear of the unrest on the land and this was something Kate also attempted when possible. The flying of the Red Ensign (Union Jack) on all ships in the British Isles was a permanent reminder of crown control. All these circumstances were the motivation for merchant seamen and families to feel more 'safe' while at sea away from the turmoil on the land.

Chapter 10

WAR

As the first decade of the twentieth century ended there were signs of unrest all over Europe. Ireland was in a state of disturbance that would reach its peak with the Easter Rising in 1916 and escalate into the War of Independence. The 1914-1918 war, the First World War, affected shipping and coasting in many ways. Coasting could be very dangerous indeed, but it could also be highly profitable, as large sums of money were offered to anyone who was willing to use their small coasters to ship cargoes of ammunition.

The Kynoch munitions factory, which had been established in Arklow in 1896, would now, due to the outbreak of war, become a most sought-after exporter. As Kate had known it would, the factory brought a great deal of shipping trade to Arklow. A ship called *Eller* was one of those to bring gun cotton to Arklow for the munitions factory. The shipping of cargo from Queensbury to the Kynoch's plant was difficult due to the hard conditions in the Arklow port which forced larger ships to discharge their cargo outside the port to be picked up by smaller boats.

This whole process took twice as long as it would had the port permitted entry to the larger vessels. It was also difficult to load cargo from the munitions factory for the outbound journey, as care had to be exercised so that when a vessel moored in the river, it would be able to sail immediately the cargo of munitions was loaded – otherwise there was a risk of explosion. This was obviously a great matter for concern to all.

One problem that was pressing on Kate's mind at this time was the troubled question of insurance. The coasting trade documents acquired by Kate specified that the ship was not insured in the event of war. The brick and tile companies in Britain and Ireland were doing very well, but Kate was painfully aware that if the *Denbighshire Lass* and her cargo were sunk due to an act of war, and no insurance was available, all her father and she had worked so hard for would be lost; she and her family would be left with nothing. She began to make sure that her children James, now fourteen, and Elizabeth, nine, learned as much as possible about the business.

While war was the major fear in 1914, the work of coasting obviously continued. Obstacles or no, problems or no, the *Denbighshire Lass* still sailed. For example, the official log book Accounts of Voyages and Crew for 1914 reads as follows:

Name	Year of Birth	Capacity	Town
John Fitzpatrick	1863	Master	Arklow
Peter Hall	1873	Mate	Arklow
James Gratton	1860	AB	Arklow
Patrick Greene	1896	Cook	Arklow

Account of Voyages

From	To
Waterford 13/02/1914	Leyavey 28/02/1914
Leyavey 25/03/1914	Ballinacurra 15/04/1914
Ballinacurra 27/04/1914	Falmouth 02/05/1914
Falmouth 14/05/1914	Highbridge 20/05/1914
Highbridge 23/05/1914	Newport 28/05/1914
Newport 31/05/1914	Tinabunnia 20/06/1914
Tinabunnia 24/06/1914	Arklow 24/06/1914
Arklow 30/06/1914	Cardiff 04/07/1914

Vessel was windbounded from January 15th until 13th February 1914.

Signed: John Fitzpatrick, 9th July 1914 (Cardiff).

Account of Voyages

Name	Year of Birth	Ship	Capacity Engaged	Town
JohnFitzpatrick	1861	Denbighshire Lass	Master	Arklow
Peter Hall	1865	Denbighshire Lass	Mate	Arklow
James Gratton	1859	Denbighshire Lass	AB	Arklow
Tom Fitzpatrick	1897	St.Theresa (Fishing)	Cook	Arklow
SamWeadock	1897	Antelope Wexford	Seamen	Arklow
Patrick Brennan	1881	S.SCoty (Belfast)	Mate	Arklow

Above names, Peter Hall discharged at Waterford and Sam Weadock discharged at Duncannon.

From	To
Arklow 01/07/1914	Cardiff 04/07/1914
Cardiff 11/07/1914	Tinabunnia 14/07/1914
Tinabunnia 20/07/1914	Newport Man 24/07/1914
Newport Man 31/07/1914	Passage East 13/08/1914
PassageEast 27/08/1914	Saunders Fort 28/08/1914
Saunders Fort 31/09/1914	Waterford 04/09/1914
Waterford 28/09/1914	Cardiff 11/10/1914
Cardiff 14/10/1914	Passage East 17/10/1914

Passage East 06/11/1914   Newport Man 08/11/1914
Newport Man 18/11/1914   Duncannon 22/11/1914
Duncannon 15/12/1914   Saunders Fort 12/01/1915

Signed: John Fitzpatrick, 12th January 1915.

So while war was threatened and coaster insurance was in question, still the trade continued and was so intense that these vessels actually worked through the winter months of September, October, November, and December. Once again John's nephew, Thomas, now seventeen, was on board, as was Laurence Brennan's son, Patrick Brennan, now twenty-three years old.

The period 1914-1918 must have been a frightening time to be on board a ship anywhere in the Irish sea, as there were stories of U-boats firing upon any craft flying the Red Ensign, as of course all Irish ships were obliged to do. Connaghs Quay, the home of schooners and ketches, would be one of the many areas of coastline damaged irretrievably by U-boats, resulting in massive coasting trade loss which would have far-reaching effects on the British Isles.

In 1916, with the war in Europe in its third year and with Ireland suffering its own turmoil, Kate was again to suffer a personal loss, when the last surviving member of her family, her sister Ellen, died on 22 December. The funeral arrangements were taken care of by John.

The loss of Kate's sister, and her own physical problems which had begun with the birth of her children, were to affect Kate badly. She had difficulty moving now. Even with her love of merchant shipping and her vessel, it took a great effort for Kate to go on board between the years 1916 and 1920. But as unwell as she may have been, she still persisted on boarding the vessel and discussing business as usual in the skipper's cabin. Her daughter

Elizabeth, now thirteen, would accompany with her now and would assist Kate with all her endeavours, helping her as she walked up the gangway. Both she and her brother James were completely at home on board the vessel – James was already sailing with his father, as can be seen on the 1918 crew lists, where he is listed as James E. Fitzpatrick. John Fitzpatrick, always a gentler personality than his wife, had more patience that Kate when teaching them the rudiments of seafaring, and often had them on board during his voyages.

In 1918 Kate finally had her longed-for changes made to her beloved ship. The *Denbighshire Lass* now had a tall mainmast and small mizzen, both rigged with gaff and boom sails. This made handling the sails much easier, and needed fewer crew. Many others schooners at the time had had these changes made.

Chapter 9

THE FINAL VOYAGES OF THE *DENBIGHSHIRE LASS*

The year 1918 finally saw the end of the First World War, the 'war to end all wars'. Ireland, however, still had her own troubles. Her ports and docks were still controlled by the Crown, but there were moves in motion to acquire an Irish national flag – the Tricolour – to replace the Red Ensign or Union Jack.

The Kynoch munitions factory, however, while thriving between the years 1914-1918, devastated Arklow in 1917, when a huge explosion killed twenty-seven of the workers. In February 1918 it was announced that the plant would close. This must have been an indescribable blow for the whole county, and to many others – so many workers had been employed in the factory, from as far away as Wexford, that special transportation had had to be laid on for them.

The closure of the plant had many repercussions for Kate's business. The continual shipping of coal to the factory from Britain had given work to many ships, and now an enormous amount of coasting business had been lost.

The *Denbighshire Lass* was now sailing as ketch rigged and was coasting again across the Irish sea on some of her normal voyages. The official Log Book of Voyage and Crew (ref. Archive Records) for early 1918 is as follows:

Name	Year of Birth	Ship	Capacity	Town
John Fitzpatrick	1863	DLass	Master	Arklow
James E. Fitzpatrick	1901	D/Lass	Mate	Arklow
Arthur Byrne	1900	Empress	AB	Arklow
Patrick Redmond	1901	Empress	Cook	Arklow

The voyages were as follows:

From	To
Waterford 18/03/1918	Cardiff 08/04/1918
Cardiff 18/04/1918	Waterford 26/04/1918
Waterford 03/05/1918	Cardiff 17/05/1918
Cardiff 27/05/1918	Waterford 07/06/1918
Waterford 18/06/1918	Cardiff 26/06/1918

Vessel under repair at Waterford 1st January-18th March 1918. Boat Drill performed and life saving equipment inspected in each port.

Signed: John Fitzpatrick (Master),
2nd July 1918.

John and Kate's son James, now eighteen years old, served as mate on this voyage; in fact this combination of master and mate was not to change for the rest of the time the *Denbighshire Lass* was to sail. Elizabeth also sailed frequently at this time.

It was a situation that may well have suited Kate. Her health was worsening considerably. Now fifty-five, in an age when people did not live as long as they do today, she was increasingly fragile and found movement more and more difficult. She was forced, reluctantly, to slow down. The latter half of the year 1918 was also a very busy time for the coasting business. The official Log Book account of Voyage and Crew reads as follows:

Name	Year of Birth	Capacity Engaged	Ship
John Fitzpatrick	1863	Master	Denbighshire Lass
James Fitzpatrick	1900	Mate	Denbighshire Lass
Edward Rourke	1852	AB	Denbighshire Lass
James Gratton	1881	Cook	Emgya Gimastin

The account of voyages for the latter half of 1918 reads as follows:

From	To
Cardiff 02/07/1918	Waterford 09/07/1918
Waterford 26/07/1918	Cardiff 02/08/1918
Cardiff 28/08/1918	Arklow 07/09/1918
Arklow 16/12/1918	Cardiff 18/01/1919

These archive records for 1918 include the following letter attached to the voyage accounts:

John Tyrrell
Ship Broker
Coal Exporter & Co.

January 22, 1919
Bute Docks, Cardiff

Superintendent of Board of Trade, Cardiff.

Dear Sir,
I arrived in Cardiff on the 18th inst. and on the next day, feeling unwell, I sent down my official Log Book and account of Crew on the Monday. I omitted to send my register and on my agent presenting the Log Book yesterday he found he had not got the register. I have only been able to come down today and bring the register with me.

Yours respectfully,
John Fitzpatrick,
Master of schooner *Denbighshire Lass*.

There was word now of a coal strike looming, something that all mariners knew would affect the coasting trade badly. In the meantime, John Fitzpatrick continued trading to Cardiff and the Bristol channel, as well as making some home-run voyages to Waterford, Cork and Dublin.

Following a reign of terror imposed on Ireland by the Black and Tans, Kate, like the far-sighted shipping owner she was, was one of the first to acquire the Irish Tricolour as a nautical flag, which she wanted to fly as soon as she could. The flag was kept locked up in the skipper's cabin. By 1921, when a truce had been called in Ireland, the Denbighshire Lass was still coasting, though Kate herself

was very unwell. The official Log Book and accounts of
Voyage and Crew for early 1921 read as follows:

Crew

Name	Year of Birth	Capacity Engaged	Ship
John Fitzpatrick	1858	Master	D/Lass
James E. Fitzpatrick	1900	Mate	D/Lass

Vessel lying up at Waterford from 1st January 1921 to 30th June 1921.

[The date of birth for John is incorrectly given as 1858; it
was in fact 1863.]

Account of Voyages

From	To
Waterford 01/07/1921	Cardiff 20/07/1921
Cardiff 05/08/1921	Youghal 26/08/1921
Youghal 10/09/1921	Cardiff 15/09/1921
Cardiff 25/09/1921	Youghal 29/09/1921
Youghal 17/10/1921	Arklow 21/10/1921

Attached to the record is the note: 'Not at sea since.'

Signed: John Fitzpatrick, 21 October 1921.

While John and son James were now sailing the vessel,
Elizabeth, now sixteen, remained at home looking after
Kate. She had become almost entirely housebound.
Physical weakness and the depression that had come over
her on the death of her sister Ellen – the last surviving
member of her immediate family – had a profound effect
on her.

During late September 1921, she became seriously ill.
Elizabeth sat with her, night after night. The responsibilities which Kate had had to take on at a very young age

may explain why perhaps she was harder on her daughter than she was on her son. According to Elizabeth, my own dear mother, Kate was very strict. Elizabeth often had to cry to get what she wanted, but often Kate would not listen and it was her husband who gave into the little girl's demands. Perhaps Kate was hard on her daughter because Elizabeth was a constant reminder of how she had nearly lost her life when giving birth. Kate had had a hard life, and could also be hurtful; whatever the reason, poor Elizabeth often bore the brunt of her anger. Perhaps this is true of the mother/daughter relationship in general. John, however, was very supportive of his daughter when disagreements occurred. Now, however, mother and daughter became closer than ever before. But towards the end of the month, Elizabeth decided that word should be sent immediately to John and James, then in Youghal on board the *Denbighshire Lass* to return home immediately. Father and son had to leave the ship in Youghal, not long after mooring, make their way to Arklow, on one of the many fast, engine-powered schooners that sailed from Cork along the east coast, to be at Kate's bedside.

When they arrived on 2 October, they were horrified to realise that Kate was so weak that she was deteriorating rapidly. Though she remained alert, it was clear that this courageous, spirited, determined little woman was losing the battle to stay alive.

In the early hours of 4 October 1921, the priest was sent for. With her husband John and her beloved children Kate and James by her side, Kate slipped quietly away. God rest her.

The death of Kate was a traumatic blow to the whole family. It was also a blow to the town of Arklow – she had been a huge part of the town's shipping life. Kate Tyrrell's funeral, on 6 October, was attended by the backbone of the seafaring fraternity from near and far, those doughty sailors who respected her as a businesswoman, a mariner and a shipowner. All the funeral arrangements were made by James and Elizabeth.

She was buried on a very cold, calm October day. The ground was laden with heavy frost; there was no wind.

After the funeral John, though in mourning, decided that he and James needed to return to Youghal, which they did on 12 October. They wanted to bring the *Denbighshire Lass*, maybe the real love of Kate's life, home to Arklow. They sailed from Youghal on 17 October 1921, mooring in Arklow on 21 October 1921. The *Denbighshire Lass* remained there until the family had decided what to be done now in the best interests of the ship, and in accordance with what they believed Kate's wishes would have been. This is the reason for the note 'Not at sea since' on the account of voyages for the time.

With Kate dead, the main force which had driven the *Denbighshire Lass* for most of its sixty-four years, in the face of great opposition, was gone. The small schooner coasting trade had all but vanished, no longer recognisable as the flourishing business of Kate's youth. There was talk of auctioning off Kate's beloved ship. Steam ships were faster, more reliable and more economic. The ship did not sail again until late 1922, when it was always crewed by John and James, and when Elizabeth herself was often on board.

During the early 20s the *Denbighshire Lass* sailed on voyages to Cardiff and Swansea, and it was on one of these voyages that the ship hoisted and sailed the Irish Tricolour, the first ship to do so in a British port.

Many of the people present in the north dock in Swansea, where this happened, did not know what the flag signified. But it caused such a stir that the authorities almost immediately began to investigate the incident. Elizabeth's account is as follows:

'The *Denbighshire* was moored in north dock, Swansea, after discharging her cargo, and was in the process of preparing to take on board her outward-bound cargo. The skipper and a crew member proceeded aft, descending below deck, to the skipper's cabin where the lock was opened on the sailor's lock-up box.

'Stored in this were some shipping registers, nautical instruments, charts, and sail-repairing equipment.

'When part of this huge box, with a lid of two feet by five, was opened it held in one compartment the specially folded and wrapped up Tricolour nautical flag.

'The flag was removed from the box and brought on deck, where it was attached to the flag rope which was already flying the *Denbighshire Lass* flying code signals NBQM. The flag was then hoisted aloft to be seen, the crew being assembled on deck for this event.

'In the area where the *Denbighshire* lay at anchor, there were many other ships – some Irish, Russian, British, and Italian. Quite a number of Italian sailors came to examine the Denbighshire as they mistakenly thought she was flying the Italian flag!'

It was not long before a crowd had gathered, and Elizabeth told me that as he watched the flag fluttering from the mast, John, the skipper, said, 'There now, Kate's last wishes have been carried out, God rest her.'

In the way her mother before her had been close to her father, Edward Tyrrell, Elizabeth was very close to her father and was very pleased to be with him on that day. Elizabeth knew all Kate's techniques on board ship and was as well versed in navigation.

The years 1922 to 1925 were the last years of the sailing

ship, and were to see the last voyage of the *Denbighshire Lass*.

John Fitzpatrick had acquired Master Mariner status during his career in merchant shipping, just as Laurence Brennan, previous skipper of the *Denbighshire Lass*, had. But during the years after Kate's death, he found himself in a world where schooners and ketches such as his were drawing to the end of their lives.

In early June 1925 the *Denbighshire Lass* was sailing to Garston, where Edward Tyrrell had died, when, some time out to sea John Fitzpatrick collapsed. His son James and Jim Brennan took over the ship. He was suffering from peritonitis, and he was reaching crisis point. Taking a craft like the Denbighshire Lass into harbour takes a great deal of time, especially the long job of locating and seconding a berth in such a place as Garston, despite the urgency of getting medical treatment for John Fitzpatrick. As soon as the ship was at anchor, John was taken ashore and rushed, in agonising pain, to hospital. He never made it. Master John Fitzpatrick died on route on 16 June 1925.

Word of the tragedy was sent to Elizabeth. She now had to face much of the responsibilities with which Kate herself had been burdened at such a young age when, in 1885, her own father had died in Garston. As Laurence Brennan had brought the body of his friend home for burial forty years before, his son Jim, and James Fitzpatrick, now brought home the body of John Fitzpatrick to his daughter.

The funeral arrangements were managed by James and Elizabeth. The register of deaths was countersigned by William New, and the funeral arrangements were finalised on 19th June 1925.

The deaths of Kate and John now forced their children to consider whether or not to continue with the *Denbighshire Lass* sailing business. The coasting business which had been the family's livelihood was now in terminal decline in the face of competition from steam – and of course, the ship herself was ageing. They kept her in harbour until early autumn, while they considered, but in late 1925 they took the decision to sell their mother's beloved ship.

The *Denbighshire Lass* slipped anchor and set sail from Arklow for the last time in late 1925 en route to her new owner in Britain. Elizabeth told me how she regretted the sight of the ship leaving the Irish coast, knowing she would never board her again. The *Denbighshire Lass* had been part of her life since the day she had been born, and it was, after all, her mother's ship. Elizabeth was very like Kate in many ways. As she and James accompanied the new owner on board to examine the ship, she insisted on taking some keepsakes from the ship before the *Denbighshire Lass* sailed away to Britain.

Upon the arrival of the *Denbighshire Lass* in Britain, she was registered in another port near her original one of Beaumaris, Anglesey. At the beginning of 1926 the ketch sailed many of her old familiar routes, from Beaumaris past Puffin island, and voyaging northwards into the Irish sea. As she passed the Anglesey landmarks of Douglas and Bull Bay and the coastline between Caernarvonshire and Angelsey, to the open Irish sea, they must have felt familiar to the old ship.

It was now sixty-nine years since her launch in 1857, but the *Denbighshire Lass* was still sailing, though her condition was such that constant repairs were needed. Of course, now being ketch rigged, she was possibly more easily controlled on some stretches of coastline with a small crew on board.

During 1926 she was to make voyages down the Bristol channel, among other routes. On the 16 March 1926, she set out from Cardiff, sailing down the river Severn, heading for the Irish sea, past the coast of south Glamorgan. As she sailed the Bristol Channel, near an area known as the Smalls, she sprang a leak. The weather was worsening and there were gale-force winds. The *Denbighshire Lass* foundered and the crew reluctantly abandoned ship. The little ketch met her watery grave in that most dangerous of areas. All three of the crew were rescued by the GWR steamer Reindeer that same ill-fated day.

When the *Denbighshire Lass* arrived at her final resting place, it was the end of almost seventy years of sailing, and the end of an era of shipping.

EPILOGUE

On the finalising of the sale of the *Denbighshire Lass*, James and Elizabeth were no longer involved with the shipping trade.

Elizabeth (Lily), my own dear mother, passed away in October 1979. God rest her. She continued to keep many mementoes of her mother's beloved ship in an old sailor's lock-up box. These included a folder marked '*Denbighshire Lass* NBQM' and nautical charts. They obviously meant a great deal to her.

Kate's son James passed from this life in 1947 at the young age of 47 years. RIP. James and Elizabeth's children are scattered between Ireland, England and America.

Laurence Brennan passed away in 1914 and is buried in Castletown, Co. Wexford.

Moses Fitzpatrick made his new home in Australia. His son was Norman Fitzpatrick (RIP). Norman's son Neil Fitzpatrick also lives in Australia, where he is a well-known actor in the theatre and in films such as *A Cry In The Dark,* where he played the judge, and television programmes such as the highly successful *Against the Wind.* He recently starred to great acclaim in Ron Blair's highly praised one-man play *The Christian Brothers,* directed by Helmut Bakaitos. Neil has also worked with the Royal Shakespeare Company and England's National Theatre during his career, as well as with all the major Australian companies. He appeared in the world premier of Tom Stoppard's *Rosencranz and Guildenstern Are Dead,* as well as plays such as *Tea and Sympathy.*

Thomas Fitzpatrick's son, also named Tom, and a man I am pleased to have spoken to many times, died at a great age recently. He left no children.

Julia Fitzpatrick, who married Mr Greene, was survived by her children William, Harriet, Nan and Tom.

I found it difficult to trace Mary Fitzpatrick's branch of the family tree, but, as far as I can ascertain, she married and lived in the outskirts of Liverpool.

During the *Denbighshire Lass*'s lifetime, 1857-1926, there would be a huge change in shipping. Steam, dating back to the Great Western paddle-propelled ship in 1838 and developing at great rates, was to become increasingly important. For some years, though, sail was to share the seas with steam, but number of sailing ships would never be seen again. Ships' engines really began to develop in 1850, with vessels like the Baltic. The same year the *Denbighshire Lass* was launched, 1857, saw 3,650-ton wooden wooden ships, such as the Adriatic, supplied with oscillating engines for power. They may have been faster and more powerful than the clippers, but they were equally dangerous – lighting came from oil and candles which had to be carefully watched, and which were a huge fire hazard. They came to be replaced by gas lighting, and later by electricity on engine-driven ships such as the 5,147-ton *Arizona,* the biggest ship to sail from Clyde.

By 1886, when the *Denbighshire Lass* began trading from Ireland, the largest shipbuilders, such as the huge

Harland & Wolfe shipyard in Belfast, were building ships solely from steel. It was the beginning of the end of sail. The facts are that during the peak sailing days of the famous clippers, all this technological advancement of engine and steam powered craft was racing ahead to replace sail power at an enormous pace.

The years 1926-1930 would see the final phasing out of sail power. Steel-built ships of 1926 had Babcock and Wilcock water tube boilers and generators of up to 400KW capacity, driven by diesel and engines.

Many artefacts from the *Denbighshire Lass* can now be seen in the Maritime Museum, Arklow. These include the ship's speed logs, the ship's folder of documents, a photograph of the ship in the Cumberland Basin and more. Kate would have been delighted.

MORE FASCINATING HISTORY TITLES FROM ATTIC PRESS AND BASEMENT PRESS

IN THEIR OWN VOICE

Women and Irish Nationalism

Margaret Ward

'Freedom for our nation and the complete removal of all disabilities to our sex will be our battle cry!' Bean na hEireann

Women such as Constance Markievicz, Maud Gonne, Hanna Sheehy-Skeffington, Louie Bennett and countless more fought for Irish independence. Collected and introduced by historian Margaret Ward, author of *Unmanageable Revolutionaries* and *Maud Gonne: A Life*, this ground-breaking collection gives us the voices of these women themselves, as they wrote in the newspapers of the day and as they explained themselves in autobiographies, letters and speeches.

The words of these women - their hopes and dreams, their terrors and their refusal to accept defeat - have for too long been buried in dusty archives. *In Their Own Voice* is a unique and invaluable collection for teachers, students and anyone interested in reclaiming Irish women's contribution to our history.

£8.99

SMASHING TIMES

A history of the Irish women's suffrage movement, 1889-1922

Rosemary Cullen Owens

While Irish nationalists were battling for Home Rule and the affairs of the Land League, Irish women were also battling for the basic right to vote.

Smashing Times brings to life the Irish women of the 1900s who were active and militant suffragists. It is a unique and enthralling account of how they fought for women's rights, particularly the right to vote, how they set about obtaining their objectives, how they were viewed by the Irish public, priests and politicians. It also examines their historic achievement and their effect on Irish society.

'Rosemary Cullen Owens has written the engrossing story of how Irish women broke through massive obstacles and achieved the vote by 1928' *Margaret MacCurtain*

£8.99

FROM DUBLIN TO NEW ORLEANS

The journey of Nora and Alice

Suellen Hoy and Margaret MacCurtain

In the autumn of 1889, Nora and Alice, two young twenty-year-old women, left the relative security of their Dominican convent boarding school at Cabra in north Dublin. They set off on a journey so far removed from their daily lives that the resulting diaries recording their adventures make engrossing reading.

The purpose of their journey was not to make their fortune but to begin a life in religion as Dominican sistersin New Orleans.

'Whether or not you were a Dominican pupil like me, you will find the story riveting' *Patricia Scanlan.*

£9.99

A LINK IN THE CHAIN

The story of the Irish Housewives Association 1942-1992

Hilda Tweedy

'During a campaign that demanded school meals for children, one reverend gentleman said that the Irish Housewives Association would be breaking up the sanctity of the home if children were to be fed at school.'

In 1942, during the 'Emergency', a group of women met to discuss the dreadful conditions in which some women and children were living. These women founded the Irish Housewives Association, an immensely influential pressure group which was to go on speaking out about injustices and the needs of Irish women, inside and outside the home, for the next fifty years.

Founder member Hilda Tweedy recalls issues as diverse as employment equality and Buy Irish campaigns in a history of a movement that has touched the lives of all Irish women over the last half century.

£5.99

EMERGING FROM THE SHADOW

The lives of Sarah Anne Lawrenson and Lucy Olive Kingston

Daisy Lawrenson Swanton

Emerging from the Shadow is the story of two generations of women. The diaries of Sarah Lawrenson and her daughter Lucy Kingston give a wonderfully atmospheric picture of life in Wicklow and Dublin - from Dalkey to Rathmines - in the late nineteenth century.

Sarah Lawrenson courageously supported herself and her husband after her husband died, leaving her with four small children; Lucy Kingston campaigned for the rights of women and for peace. She became involved in the suffrage movement, the Women's International League for Peace and Freedom, and CND. Her story is full of personal social detail and political history.

£10.99